Sylvia Rodger
1975

The Art of Needlegraph

by Sylvia Goldman

The Art of Needlegraph

At last—patterns that let you create your own masterpieces, using your own colors, wools and stitches.

ACKNOWLEDGMENTS

To my husband Murray, and my children: Steven, David, Gary, and Tina, for their love and encouragement.

To my friends and volunteers: Irene Braun, Ellen Conovitz, Bobby Dean, Judy Einsidler, Sara Gerstein, Isabel Goldman, Miriam Grossman, Gail Harris, Sophie Hauptman, Ruth Koeppel, Arlene Lieberman, Florence Margolies, Ellie Mendelsohn, Gail Nick, Miriam Nissenbaum, Ellen Ross, Shirley Trencher, and Arlene Wolff, my thanks and sincere appreciation for their invaluable help in working out the samples in this book.

To Adrienne Gordon of "Open Door to Stitchery" in Great Neck, Long Island, New York, for her help and assistance in making this book a reality.

Finally, to Ruth Saks, who started it all.

Designed by HAROLD FRANKLIN

distributed by Book Sales Inc.,
110 Enterprise Avenue
Secaucus, N. J. 07094

ISBN 0-89009-025-4

Library of Congress catalogue card number 74-76259

MANUFACTURED IN THE UNITED STATES OF AMERICA

In Loving Memory to My Beloved Daughter,
Deborah Lee Goldman,
October 13, 1954—September 24, 1971

"In this sad world of ours, sorrow comes to all . . .
it comes with bitterest agony . . .
Perfect relief is not possible, except with time.
You cannot now realize that you will ever feel better . . .
And yet this is a mistake. You are sure to be happy again.
To know this, which is certainly true,
will make you some less miserable now.
I have had experience enough to know what I say."

Abraham Lincoln

INTRODUCTION

This is not a book on how to do needlepoint. It is a book for the person who already knows the basics of this craft and wants to take it another step further. That next step is Needlegraph. Needlegraph is count stitchery: following a graph, box by box, to create a design.

These designs I have created are geometric, with two thoughts in mind, simplicity and color. The charts are simple to follow, with detailed instructions for each pattern. The designs have been arranged in the order of their simplicity, the easiest first and ending with the more challenging ones. Try a fairly uncomplicated design for your first attempt at Needlegraph. •

GENERAL INSTRUCTIONS

These designs can be worked into other methods of needlework. Cross-stitch embroidery, punch hooking etc., pillows, rugs, benches, seat covers, whatever your creative mind wishes.

As far as color is concerned, if you love a design but they are not your colors, simply replace my colors for yours. At the yarn store combine your colors in natural light if possible, if they look well together they will work out well together.

Once you have selected the design you are going to do, a handy idea to follow would be to photostat the design. It is easier to handle and it folds nicely into your work bag. If the charts in the book are not large enough, you can have them photostated and enlarged. Another marvelous and simple reason why you should have the pattern photostated is, when you are ready to work the second half of the pattern, the pattern has to be reversed. A helpful hint is to turn the photostat to the reverse side and put it up to the light. Now you have the pattern in reverse and going in the proper direction. Each graph is a quarter of the complete design.

MARKING AND FOLLOWING A GRAPH

Mark the horizontal and vertical center lines on your canvas all the way down and across with waterproof pen. This way you will always know where the center is as the yarn covers the canvas. The center of your canvas is where the two lines intersect. An X marks the center of each graph, this X corresponds with the center of your canvas. Note that on each graph in this book I have marked the starting square with a RED X.

Each box stitch of the graph represents a crossing of a horizontal and a vertical canvas thread of the stitch which will cover it, NOT THE HOLE BETWEEN THREADS. Simply, one graph box= one stitch.

Mark TOP on top of your canvas in case the design has a one way pattern, also, you will always know which way your stitch should go.

RULES

Geometric designs are easy to do if you follow some simple rules. Always start at the center of the pattern.

Work a section at a time, working your way out to the edges.

If the design has an outline, do the outline first. Once the outline is done the most important counting is out of the way, then you can fill in the pattern.

The background is the last to be done.

The most important rule to remember in Needlegraph is to continuously refer to your chart every few stitches to see if the work you have done so far corresponds with the chart. Unfortunately one stitch that is wrong will throw your design completely off. So if you check often you can rectify errors immediately without too much trouble.

Once you are familiar with the design while working, you get into a certain rhythm and once that rhythm is established, it becomes so very simple.

CANVAS AND YARN

Purchase the best quality canvas and yarn available as this is the foundation of your work. Buy all your wool at one time, especially the background color to avoid any changes in dye lots. It is better to buy a little more than you may need than to be caught short.

I have used 10 to the inch graph and canvas for many reasons. #10 mono canvas is excellent for most needlepoint. It is easier on the eyes and easier to count the lines. It will allow you to finish a project in a reasonable time. Geometrics do not need any fine detailing, but if you prefer to use another size canvas, keep in mind that it will change the size of your project. All sizes given in this book are approximate.

MATERIALS

For chart reading I have found a magnifying glass very helpful.

Small sharp pointed scissors with a 36″ length of yarn or ribbon attached to them at the handles, make it easy to hang them around your neck and always have them available when needed.

Also, my best friend, the thimble. Try to get used to one as it saves wear and tear on your fingers.

PREPARING THE CANVAS

Cut a piece of canvas that is at least two inches wider on all sides of the design you have selected. For instance, a 12″ x 12″ design needs a 16″ x 16″ canvas. You will need the surplus canvas for blocking. Tape all sides with one inch masking tape to prevent raveling.

Center your pattern by folding the canvas in half, then in half again. Mark the horizontal and vertical center lines. I use the Sharpie Waterproof Pen that can be found in most *Five and Tens* and certainly in any art supply store. It is the only one that I have found that hasn't run on me yet. Use it lightly as the very pale colors sometimes don't cover completely.

RUGS AND CARPETING

Rugs worked in sections are easier to handle and carry around with you, then joined together with the Binding stitch. The sections should be blocked separately and be perfectly square before joining together. The Binding stitch is the easiest and most inexpensive way to seam canvas together. It is also used for finishing raw edges as well. Be sure to match mesh to mesh when joining together so the sides come out evenly.

You can use #3, 5, 7, and #10 canvas for your rugs. If you use #5 canvas and rug yarn, your measurements will be double the measurements quoted for #10 canvas. For example, a graph using #10 canvas shows the finished size to be 12″ x 12″, the finished piece using #5 canvas will be 24″ x 24″. If you should want to make a rug measuring 24″ x 48″, all you have to do is make another section exactly alike and bind together.

Using #10 canvas is my preference as the finished piece has a finer look and finish. But whatever your choice, any one of the patterns shown in this book, even the round ones, (by squaring off the design), can be easily transformed into carpet size.

QUICK POINT PILLOWS

The same rule applies to quick-point pillows when using #5 canvas. Your finished measurement will be approximately twice the size for a design using #10 canvas. Just make sure to use heavier yarn so the canvas is covered completely.

STITCHES TO USE

I have used the Basketweave Stitch throughout this book. Knowing this Stitch lends itself to outlining the patterns and filling in the designs. But for the backgrounds, there are many stitches that would lend themselves beautifully. On "Pagoda" (page 71), for example, I used the Mosaic stitch on the border and the Double Cross Stitch as accents in the design. A few of the designs such as in "Blue Medley" (page 43), it is best to do the background in the Basketweave or the Continental Stitch if that is your preference, as the pattern is close. "Collage in Blue" (page 107) would be a good example of a pattern where the background could be done in any of your favorite stitches. Experiment with one of the many stitches available, doing this can add more interest to your work and make it truly original. In other words—do your own thing.

Work loosely so as not to pull the work out of shape, it will also be much easier to block later. Always clip off excess yarns as you work. Save one strand of each color yarn that you have used so that after your work has been blocked and finished, you can tuck the yarn into the pillow. This way you will always have the exact shade handy in case repairs ever have to be made.

A final touch to your work before you block: Needlepoint two rows of stitches in the same color yarn as the color you will line your work in. It covers the canvas when turning your work right side out as explained in the chapter "MAKING A PILLOW" (see page 11).

BLOCKING YOUR WORK

After finishing, your design will have to be blocked. No matter how carefully you work, there is likely to be some distortion. Choose a clean piece of Plywood, a bed board comes in handy if you are going to block more than one canvas or if blocking a small rug, or a long item. Tape brown paper on to the wood. Outline the measurements of your needlepoint on the paper with a Sharpie

Waterproof Pen. Use that outline as a guide for blocking. Place your needlepoint face down on the outline. Tack with non-rusting pins or tacks. I use push pins, they are easy to hammer in and to pull out.

Starting with the upper right hand corner of your canvas, use a tack every few inches. Pull and tug with a firm and strong hand, to straighten the canvas until it lines up to the outline on the brown paper. Working gradually one side then the other, until all sides are completely tacked. Now dampen with a clean wet sponge. Let the canvas stay stretched on the board for at least two days.

When dry, steam the back of the canvas with a steam iron. If canvas needs additional blocking, use a wet cloth on top of canvas and press with the steam iron. Dry. Remove tacks.

MACHINE STITCHING

After the canvas has been blocked, run a line of machine stitches or zig-zag stitches as close as possible to the worked area. Stitch all around the needlepoint a few times. This will prevent your canvas from raveling. Trim to within an inch of the unworked excess canvas on all four sides, mitering the corners within a half inch of the finished work. You are now ready to sew the fabric to your needlepoint.

MAKING A PILLOW

With the insides out, pin your fabric to your needlepoint piece. Sew the pieces together with the needlepoint on top, so that you can stitch a seam in between the double row of needlepoint stitches that I spoke of in the section "STITCHES TO USE" (see page 10).

Running that seam in between the stitches prevents the raw canvas from showing thru when you turn your casing right side out. Sew three sides and an inch on each side of the fourth side. Remove the pins and trim any excess fabric and turn right side out. Reach inside cover and push the corners out. Fill with a muslin covered pillow. Pin unsewn sides together and slip-stitch together.

CONTENTS

EASY DESIGNS

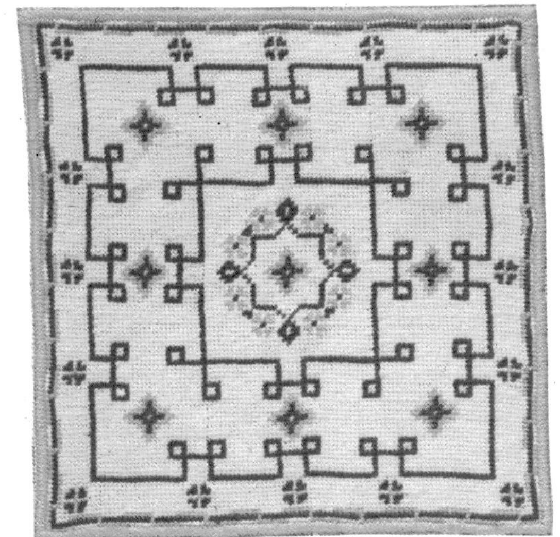

COLORS:

Purple
Royal Blue
Apple Green

White background

"ICE CRYSTALS"

DESIGN #1

12"x 12"

page 31

Shocking Pink
Apple Green
Sunshine Yellow
Bright Orange

White background

"MANDARIN SCROLLS"

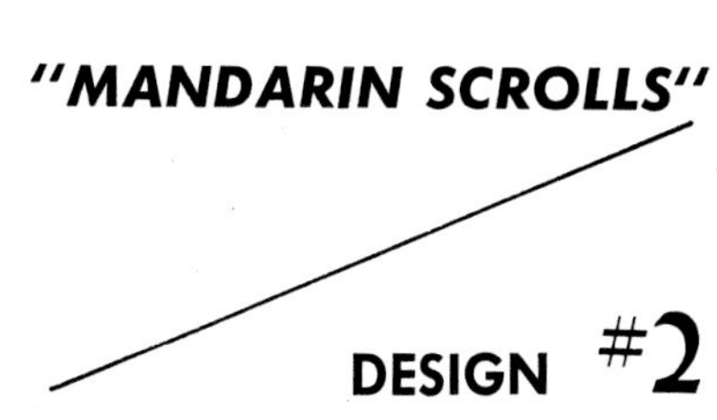

DESIGN #2

12"x 14"

page 33

Hot Pink
Turquoise Blue
Purple
Orange
Bright Yellow
Royal Blue

"PYRAMIDS"

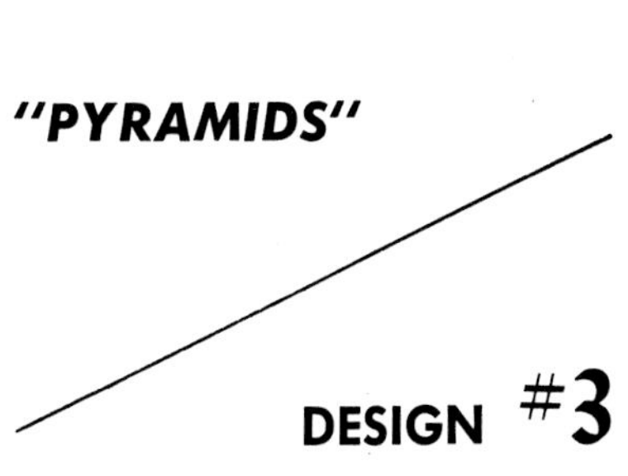

DESIGN #3

11"x 15½"

page 35

COLORS:

Orange
Deep Turquoise Blue
Black

White background

"CHIPPENDALE"

DESIGN #4

14″x 14″

page 37

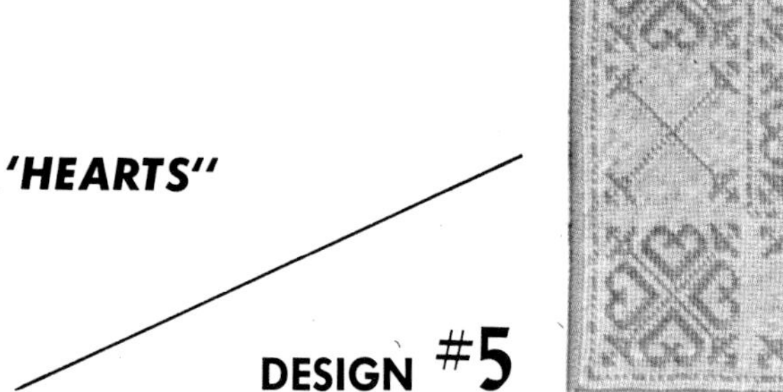

Pink
Light Blue
Yellow
Apple Green

White background

'HEARTS"

DESIGN #5

14½″x 14½″

page 39

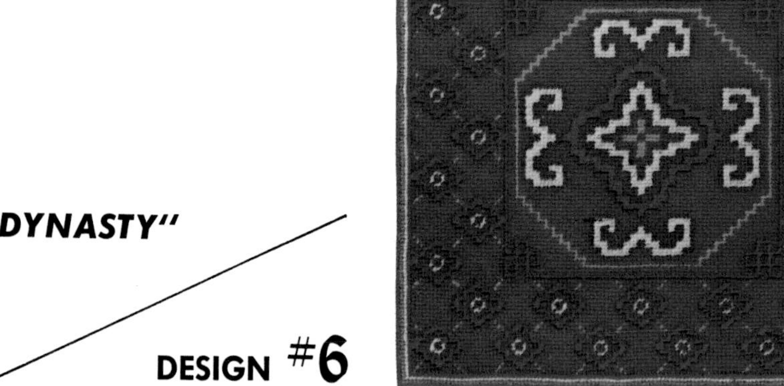

Bright Red
Buttercup Yellow
Emerald Green

Bright Blue background

"DYNASTY"

DESIGN #6

SIZE: 13″x 13″

page 41

COLORS:

White
Light Blue
Darker Blue

"BLUE MEDLEY"

DESIGN #7

13″x 14″

page 43

Pink
Bright Gold
Emerald Green

White and
Apple Green backgrounds

"CARNATIONS IN THE PINK"

DESIGN #8

15″x 15″

page 45

Dark Green
Light Green
Lavender
Pink

Yellow background

"FOUR TULIPS"

DESIGN #9

15″ x 15″

page 47

COLORS:

"GEOMETRIC"

DESIGN #10

Royal Blue
Canary Yellow
Green

White background

16″x 16″

page 49

"FLORA"

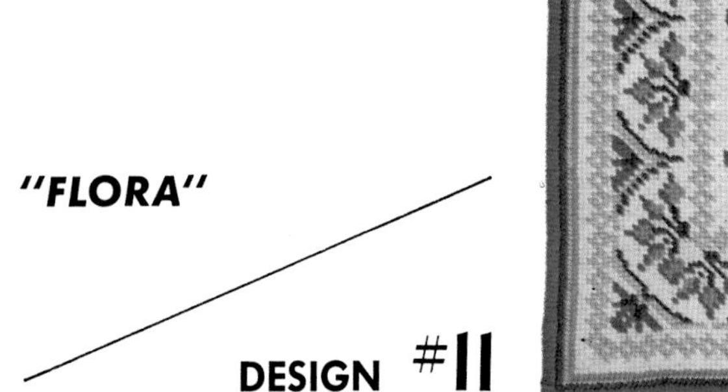

DESIGN #11

Deep Red
Coral
Dark Green
Lime Green

White background

12″x 12″

page 51

"PLUMES"

DESIGN #12

Bright Yellow
Turquoise Blue
Orange

Celery background

14″x 14″

page 53

COLORS:

"OCTAGON"

DESIGN #13

Turquoise Blue
Bright Yellow
Fire Red

White background

12″ x 12″

page 55

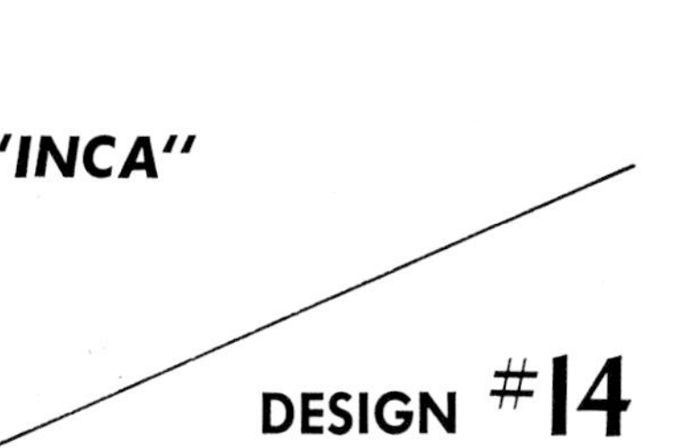

"INCA"

DESIGN #14

Lemon Yellow
Cerise
Purple
Turquoise Blue
White

12″ x 12½″

page 57

"YANGTZE SWIRLS"

DESIGN #15

Black
Orange
Yellow

White background

13″ x 13″

page 59

COLORS:

"ISTANBUL"

DESIGN #16

Black
Plum
Royal Blue
Apple Green

Lemon Yellow background

13″x 13″

page 61

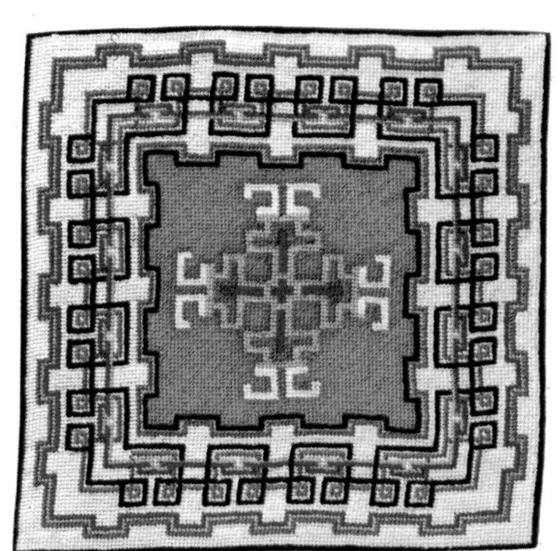

"CHINESE KEY"

DESIGN #17

Black
Yellow
Emerald Green
Orange

White background

14″x 14″

page 63

"FLEUR-DE-LIS"

DESIGN #18

Purple
Yellow
Lime Green
Dark Green
Orange
White

Orange and White backgrounds

16″x 16″

page 65

COLORS:

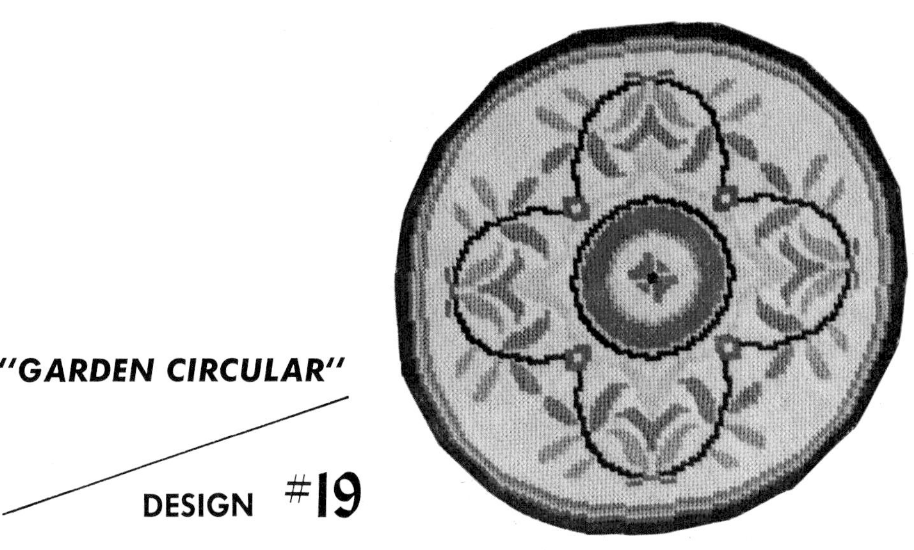

"GARDEN CIRCULAR"

DESIGN #19

Bright Yellow
Black
Olive Green
Chartreuse
Orange
White

12″ x 12″

page 67

"SNOW FLAKE"

DESIGN #20

Black
White
Chocolate Brown

Gold background

15″ x 15″

page 69

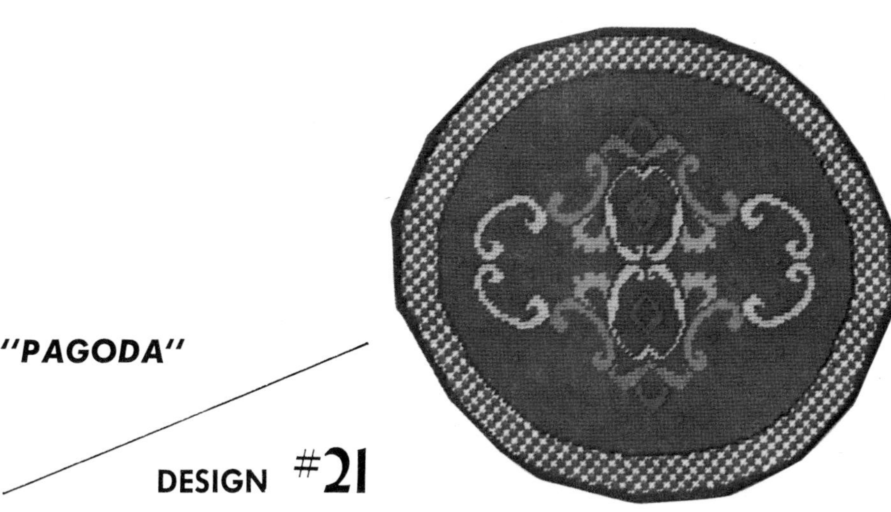

"PAGODA"

DESIGN #21

Red
Chartreuse
Lavender
Light Green
Dark Green
Yellow
Cerise

Black borders
White and
Royal Blue backgrounds

12″ x 14″

page 71

COLORS:

"BLUE DELFT"

DESIGN #22

Dark Blue
Medium Blue
Light Blue
White

13″x 15″

page 73

"TIBET"

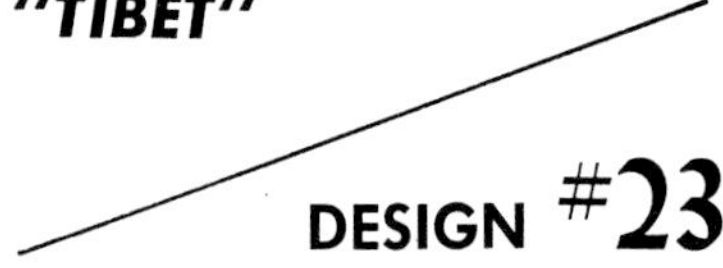

DESIGN #23

Bright Red
Black
Bright Yellow
Emerald Green

14″x 14″

page 75

"PATCHWORK"

DESIGN #24

Orange
Deep Turquoise Blue
Black

White background

12½″x 12½″

page 77

INTERMEDIATE DESIGNS

COLORS:

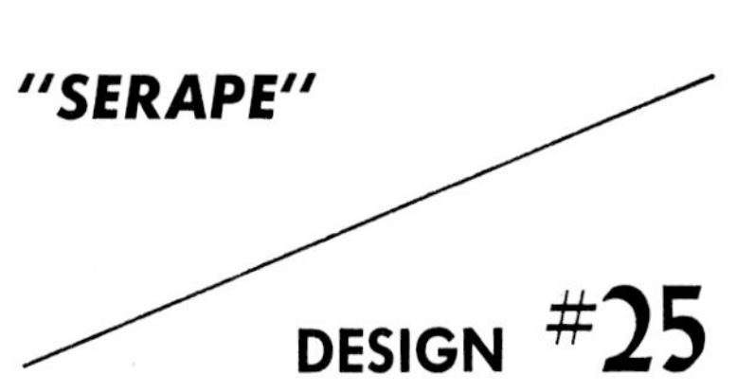

"SERAPE"

DESIGN #25

Black
Yellow
Dark Green
White
Orange
Royal Blue
Lime Green

10″x 14″

page 81

"OMAR KHAYYAM"

DESIGN #26

Navy
Gold
Emerald Green
Fire Red

16″x 16″

page 83

"XOCHIMILCO"

DESIGN #27

Yellow
Green
Purple
Orange
Blue

Black borders

14″x 14″

page 85

COLORS:

Green
Yellow
Coral

White background

"RENAISSANCE"

DESIGN #28

15″x15″

page 87

Orange
Red
Dark Green
Light Green
Dark Blue
Light Blue
Yellow

White background

"FIESTA"

DESIGN #29

14½″x14½″
ROUND

page 89

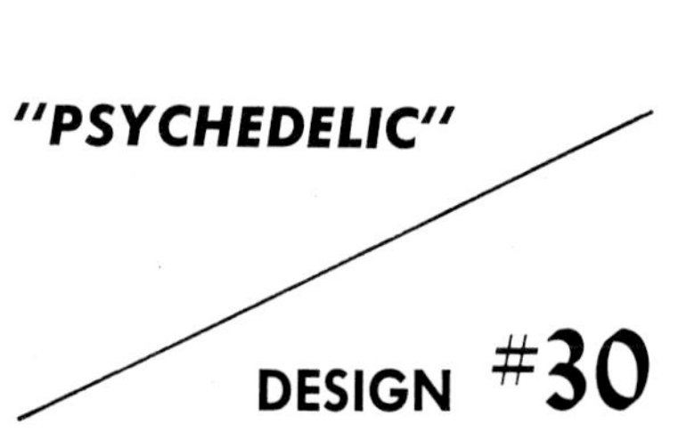

Hot Pink
Red
Light Green
Dark Green
Burgundy

White background

"PSYCHEDELIC"

DESIGN #30

14″x14″

page 91

COLORS:

Light Gold
Green
Black
Dark Gold
Bright Red

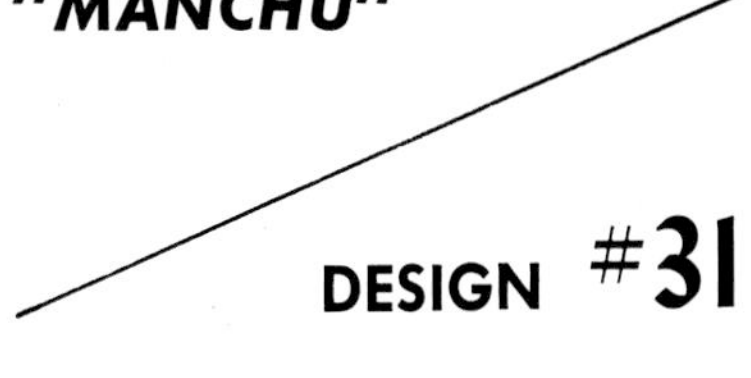

"MANCHU"

DESIGN #31

14″x 15″

page 93

Salmon
Powder Blue
Bright Green
Strong Yellow

Darker Blue and
White backgrounds

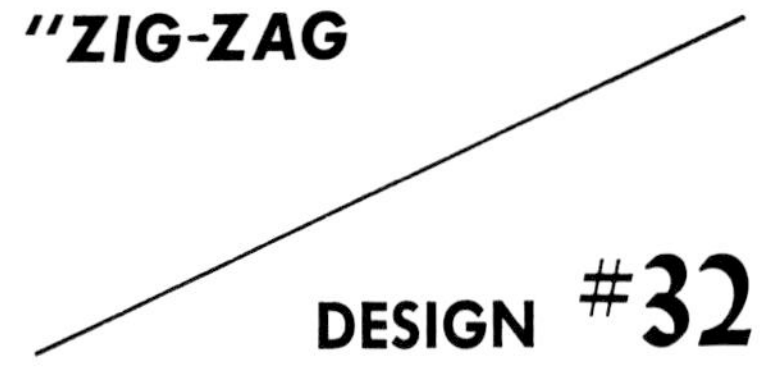

"ZIG-ZAG

DESIGN #32

14½″x14½″

page 95

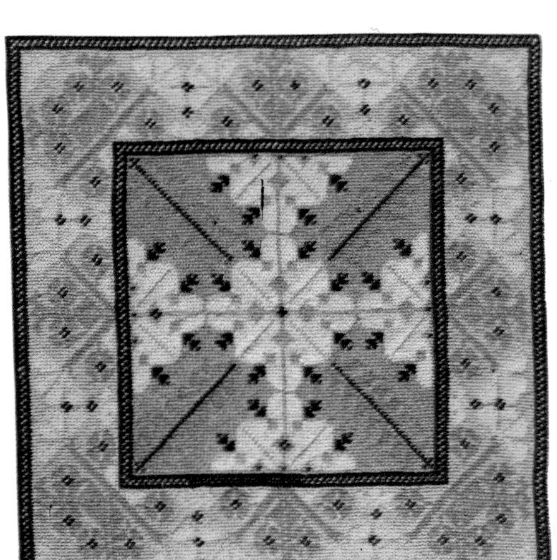

Gold
Brown
Medium Blue

Light Blue and
Melon backgrounds

"ILLUSION"

DESIGN #33

17″x 17″

page 97

COLORS:

Red
Yellow
Hot Pink
Orange
Black
White
Emerald Green

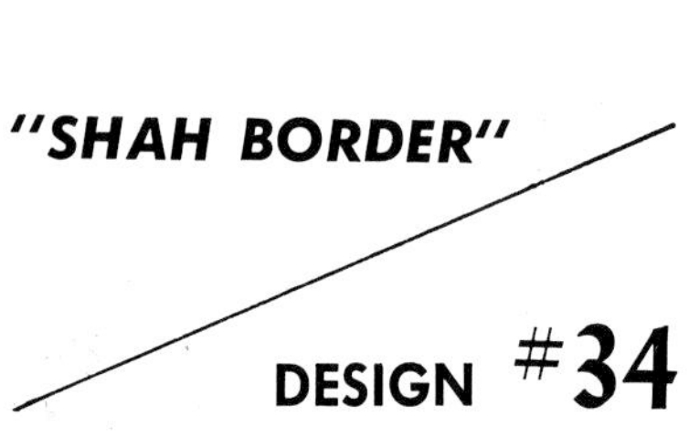

"SHAH BORDER"

DESIGN #34

15″x 15″

page 99

Black
Yellow
White
Royal Blue
Orange
Green
Plum

"PERSIAN CARPET"

DESIGN #35

12″x 12″

page 101

Red
Bright Yellow

Black background

"CHUNGKING"

DESIGN #36

16″x 16″

page 103

"ACAPULCO"

DESIGN #37

COLORS:

Hot Pink
Yellow
Lime Green
Orange
Purple

16″x 18″

page 105

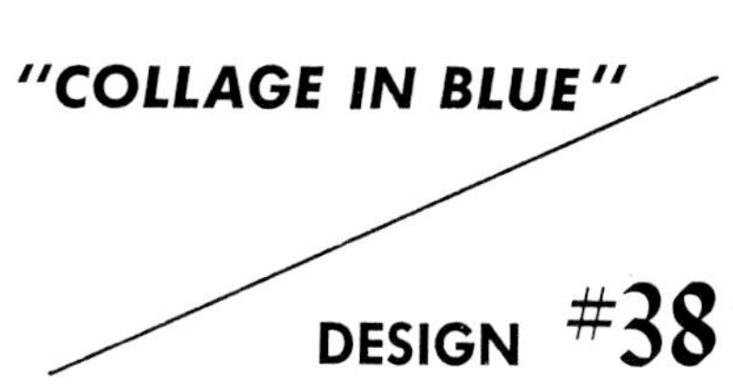

"COLLAGE IN BLUE"

DESIGN #38

White
Deep Turquoise Blue

Black outlined
Pale Turquoise Blue background

13″x 20″

page 107

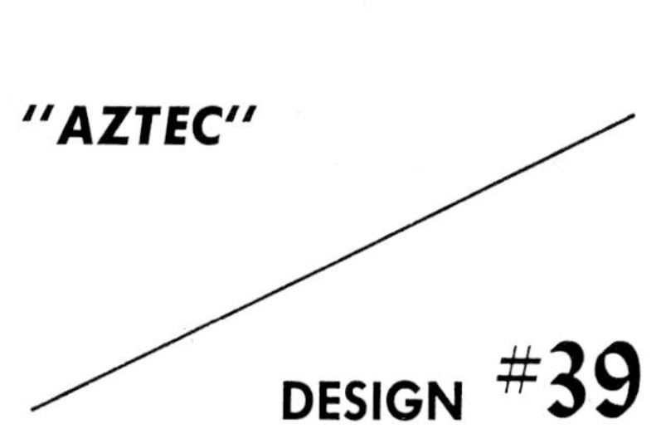

"AZTEC"

DESIGN #39

Rust Orange
Blue Grey
Bright Gold
Beige
Eggshell
Black
Medium Blue
White

12″x 16½″

page 109

COLORS:

Black
Yellow
Red
Green

"ORIENTAL BELLS"

DESIGN #40

15″ x 15″

page 111

ADVANCED DESIGNS

Shocking Blue
Cerise
Light Blue
Royal Blue
Orange

Yellow and Bright Green backgrounds

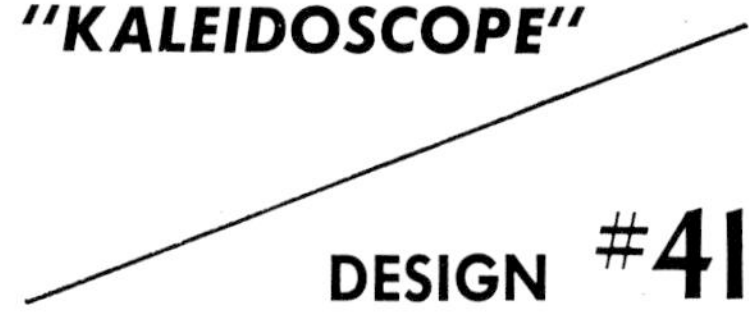

"KALEIDOSCOPE"

DESIGN #41

12½″ x 12½″

page 115

Medium Brown
Gold Yellow
Orange
Medium Blue
Sand

Bright Green and Sand backgrounds

"YUCATAN"

DESIGN #42

14″ x 14″

page 117

COLORS:

Purple
Lavender
Red
Gold
Yellow
Dark Brown
Light Brown
Light Green

White background

"PEKING AUTUMN"

DESIGN #43

16″x 16″

page 119

Red
Yellow
Black
White

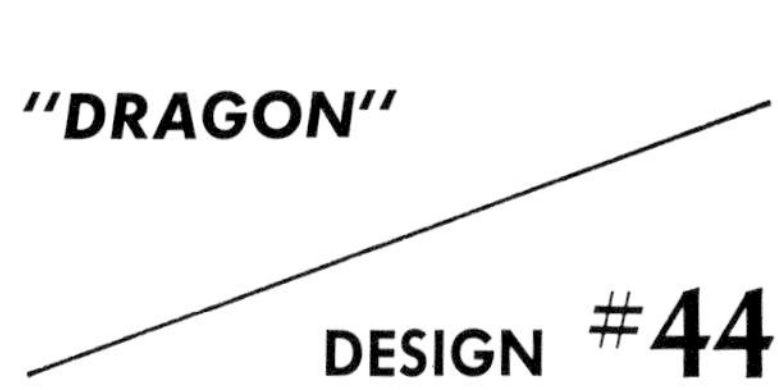

"DRAGON"

DESIGN #44

11″x 13″

page 121

Green
Brown
Yellow
Cream
Beige

"ACORN"

DESIGN #45

16½″x 16½″

page 123

Easy Designs

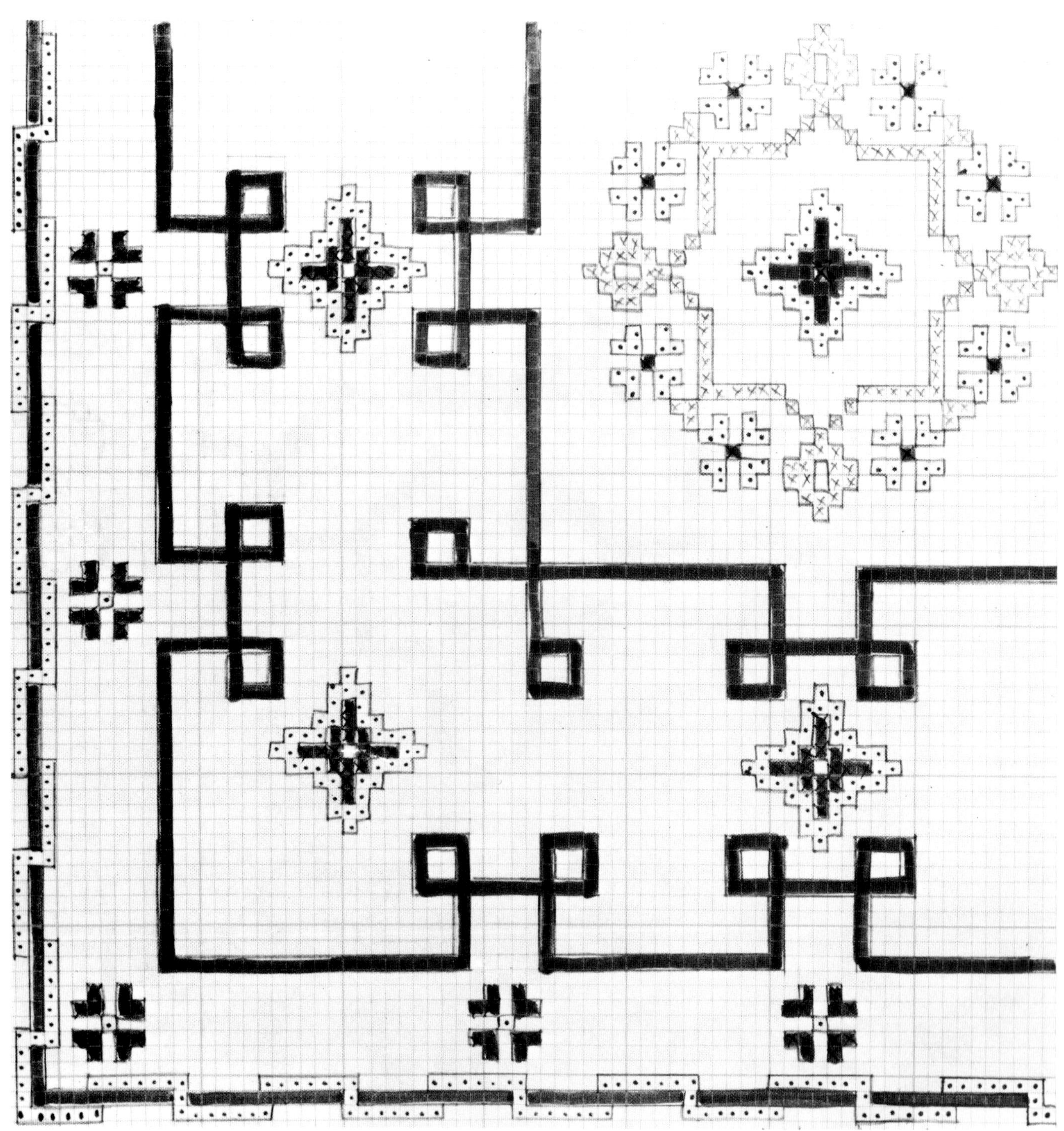

COLORS:

- ■ Purple
- ☒ Royal Blue
- ⊡ Apple Green

White background

"ICE CRYSTALS"

1. Start with the purple cross.
2. Outline the cross in apple green.
3. Do purple outline.
4. Fill in with the green flowers and dot each flower with a blue stitch.
5. Do purple border under wreath.
6. Next do the other purple border underneath.
7. Now do your green and blue flowers in between the two borders.
8. Do the purple and green border.
9. Now you can do your blue flower with the green center.
10. A nice finish to this pattern would be to make a row of each color, all around, to tie in the colors. Or a green border over three threads.
11. Now you can do your background.

SIZE: 12"x 12"

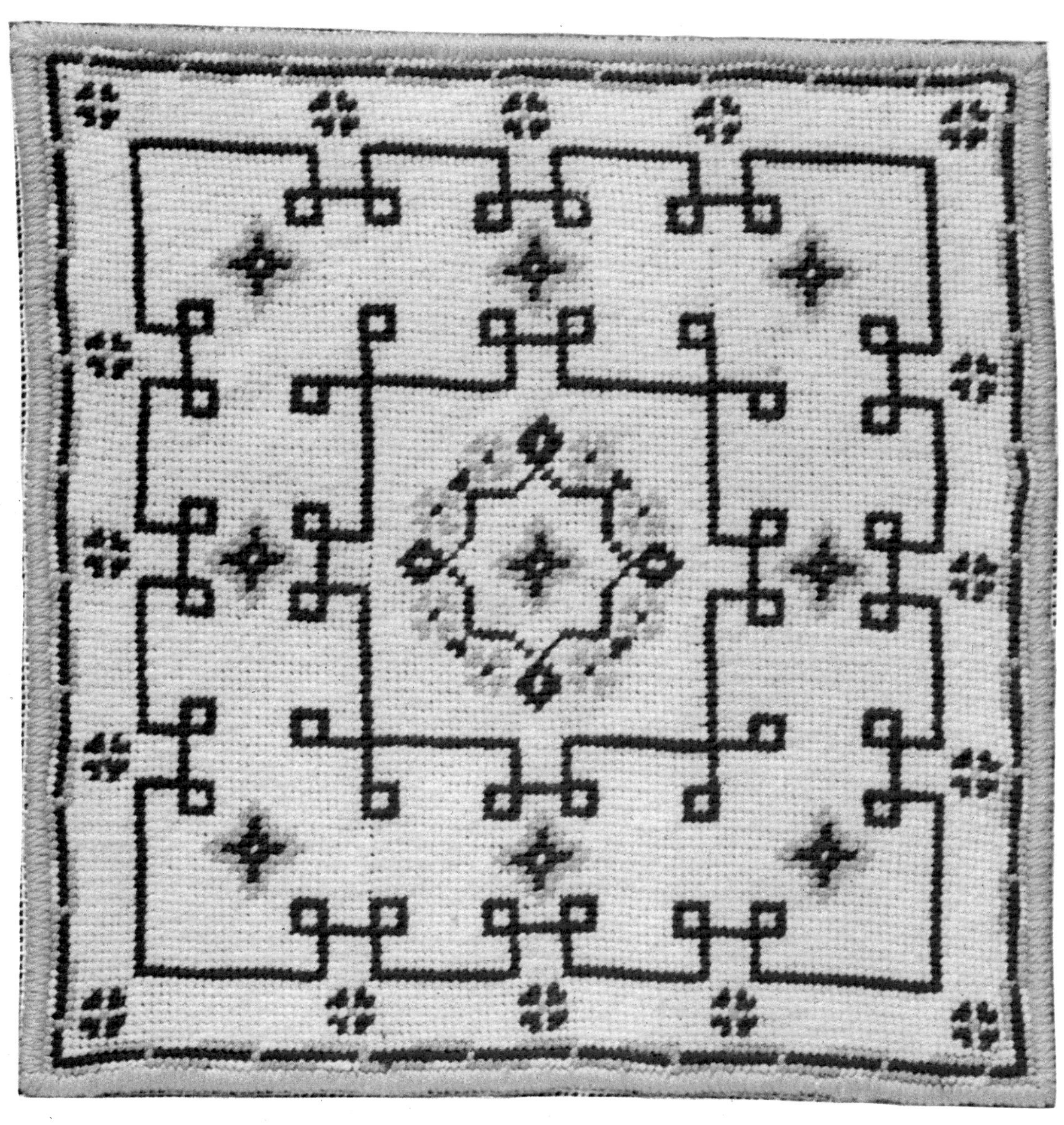

COLORS:

- ⁄ **Shocking Pink**
- ☒ **Apple Green**
- ▣ **Sunshine Yellow**
- ⊡ **Bright Orange**

White background

"MANDARIN SCROLLS"

1. Do your center yellow outline first.
2. Now the pink outline.
3. You can fill in with the orange.
4. Do your green border, starting on the sixth row under your center flower.
5. Now you can make the pink corners.
6. Repeat the same procedure as for the center flower, one at a time, making sure to center as in the graph. Adding the green loops to each flower, as each flower is completed.
7. Make a border tying in all the colors used. Using one, two or three threads as desired.
8. Fill in your background with white yarn.

SIZE: 12″x 14″

TOP

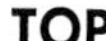

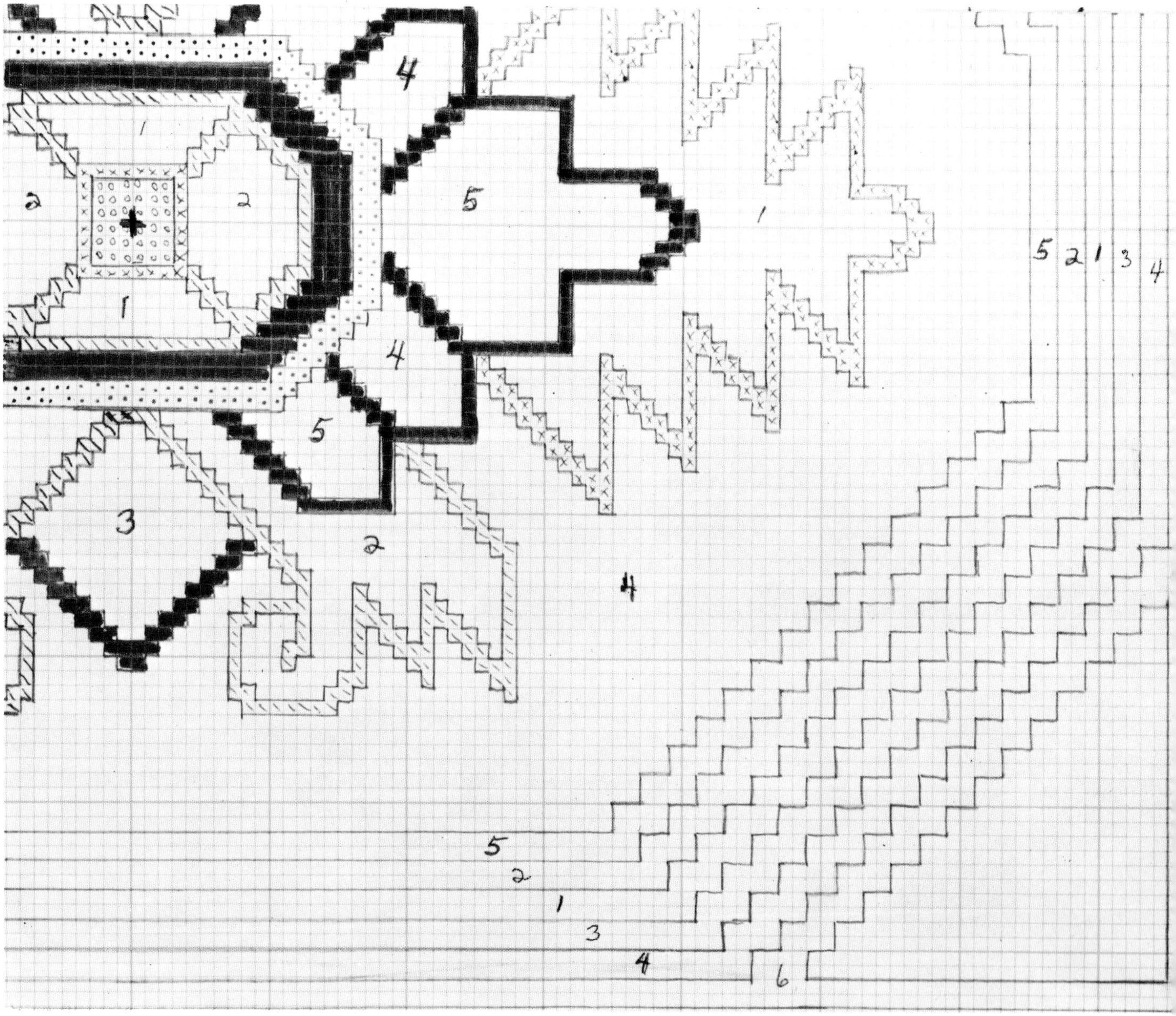

COLORS:

1 ⊡ Hot Pink
2 □ Turquoise Blue
3 ☒ Purple
4 ⊙ Orange
5 ◪ Bright Yellow
6 ■ Royal Blue

"PYRAMIDS"

1. Start with your purple square center.
2. Fill in square center.
3. Do yellow outline.
4. Fill in outline with turquoise and hot pink as indicated in graph.
5. Next do the royal blue around the yellow.
6. Put a hot pink border around the royal blue.
7. Branch out with the royal blue outlines.
8. Fill in the outlines with the yellow and orange as indicated.
9. Branch out in the yellow and fill in with the turquoise.
10. Outline the other branches, then fill in with proper colors.
11. Do six borders, one of each color.
12. Fill in each corner with hot pink, purple, yellow, and turquoise. Each corner a different color.
13. Orange background last.

SIZE: 11″x 15½″

TOP

COLORS:

- ◘ **Orange**
- ☑ **Deep Turquoise Blue**
- ■ **Black**

White background

"CHIPPENDALE"

1. Start at the center orange motif. Do outline first, then fill in.
2. Blue and orange arrows.
3. Blue scroll, starting from center to center.
4. Black border, the center one.
5. Corner orange and blue arrows.
6. Orange motif on the border starting with the center one first.
7. Then the corner motif.
8. Finally work the edge black border again starting from the center and working your way around.
9. Your background in white.

SIZE: 14″x 14″

COLORS:

- ▱ Pink
- ⊡ Light Blue
- ☒ Yellow
- ■ Apple Green

White background

'HEARTS''

1. Work your four green arrows in the center first.
2. Next do the pink hearts in between arrows.
3. The green border, starting in the center and working around.
4. Repeat the arrows and hearts, alternating blues and yellows as indicated in the pattern.
5. Repeat the green border as before.
6. Now the last green border, working over one, two, or three threads as wished.
7. Finally your white background.
8. This is a great pattern for a child's room.

SIZE: 14½″x14½″

COLORS:

- ■ Bright Red
- ⊡ Buttercup Yellow
- ⊠ Emerald Green

Bright Blue background

1. Start with your green cross in the center.
2. Work the yellow around the green cross.
3. Do the red around the yellow.
4. Start your yellow motif two rows underneath the red, in the center, working one half then the other half.
5. Green border, starting in the center.
6. Red border, two rows underneath the green border.
7. Now start your border pattern by first doing the red border closest to the edge of the design. Counting carefully twenty-six rows.
8. It will now be easier to work in your pattern between the red borders. Start with the red centers, then work the edges.
9. Yellow centers.
10. Tie in your red pattern with the green.
11. Yellow border underneath the worked red one.
12. Green border, underneath the yellow border.
13. Your final red border.
14. Finally your background in a bright blue that will complement the other colors.

SIZE: 13″x 13″

COLORS:

- ⊡ White
- ■ Light Blue
- ☒ Darker Blue

1. Start with your light blue pattern in the center where the X is.
2. Now do the dark blue pattern, starting in the center and working your way around to the edges.
3. Do all four dark blue patterns before starting with the light blue pattern.
4. Now do the light blue pattern inside the worked pattern. Starting in the center of each diamond.
5. Complete the rest of the light blue motifs in this area.
6. Light blue border, starting from the center, and working your way around.
7. White border under the light blue border.
8. Begin your outer border with the four light blue crosses in the center of the graph. Do all the crosses on the border.
9. Now work the white pattern in between.
10. Start your light blue border as in direction number six. One row.
11. One row of dark blue.
12. One row of white.
13. The middle background is done in white.
14. The border background is finished in the dark blue.
15. Make sure your blues are selected from the same family so as not to clash with each other.

SIZE: 13″x 14″

COLORS:

- ■ **Pink**
- ⊡ **Bright Gold**
- ◿ **Emerald Green**

White and Apple Green backgrounds

"CARNATIONS IN THE PINK"

EASY DESIGN #8

1. Starting in the center do the pink first.
2. Work the gold around the pink.
3. Now the pink sections underneath the gold.
4. Tie in your pink together with the emerald green
5. Do the emerald green design.
6. Start your flower with the gold stems that works itself into a border. Begin in the centers and work your way around to the corners.
7. The green base of the flower.
8. The pink flower itself.
9. Starting in the center, do the gold outline.
10. Do the gold outline on the border, starting from the center. Do the top and then the bottom gold outline.
11. Do the emerald green outline around the flower.
12. Now work the flower, starting with the gold stem, and working your way up to the gold tip.
13. The pink leaf design in the center of the gold outline.
14. The edge border in pink. Do two rows.
15. The entire center inside the gold border is done in white.
16. The area inside the outer edge, in between the pink edge border and the bottom gold outline, is also done in white.
17. The area inside the border that remains is completed in a pale green.

SIZE: 15"x15"

COLORS:

- ■ Dark Green
- ◿ Light Green
- ⊡ Lavender
- ⊠ Pink

Yellow background

"FOUR TULIPS"

1. Begin with the light green cross in the center.
2. Do the dark green around the cross.
3. Start your lavender in the middle and work your way down.
4. Fill in with the pink design.
5. Do all four dark green outlines.
6. Now fill in with the light green pattern.
7. Work your dark green border, starting from the center.
8. Complete the pattern inside the border with the pink and lavender crosses.
9. Begin your light green outline from the center.
10. Do your pink in the center of the outline.
11. Complete your pattern with the lavender around the pink.
12. Connect the patterns with the dark green.
13. Dark green border.
14. Yellow background.

SIZE: 15″x15″

COLORS:

- ■ **Royal Blue**
- ⊡ **Canary Yellow**
- ◿ **Green**

White background

"GEOMETRIC"

1. Do your blue outline starting in the center.
2. The yellow design in the center.
3. Fill in the pattern with the green.
4. Starting from the center, do the four outlines first.
5. Green centers.
6. Yellow bars.
7. Green pattern with the yellow centers.
8. Blue border.
9. Do all the blue outline work on the border pattern before filling in the design.
10. Yellow inside the blue outline.
11. Do all the green work including the center motif.
12. Complete motif with the yellow centers.
13. Blue border.
14. Yellow border.
15. Double green border, worked over two threads.

SIZE: 16″x 16″

COLORS:

- Deep Red
- Coral
- Dark Green
- Lime Green

White background

"FLORA"

1. Work the red and coral center.
2. Outline the green stems with dark green wool.
3. Fill in stems with the dark green.
4. Outline Carnations in red.
5. Fill in Carnations in coral.
6. Start working lime green flower border from the centers to the corners.
7. Next work the Pyramids, centering each one between the flower pots, and starting with the dark green yarn.
8. Follow through with your lime green, finishing the Pyramid with the red.
9. Center your flower pots, starting with the dark green and working to the corners.
10. Repeat your flower border as in step six.
11. Begin your border with the red.
12. Coral is next.
13. Lime green.
14. Finally your dark green.
15. This border can be worked over one, two, or three threads if desired.
16. Do your background in white.

SIZE: 12"x 12"

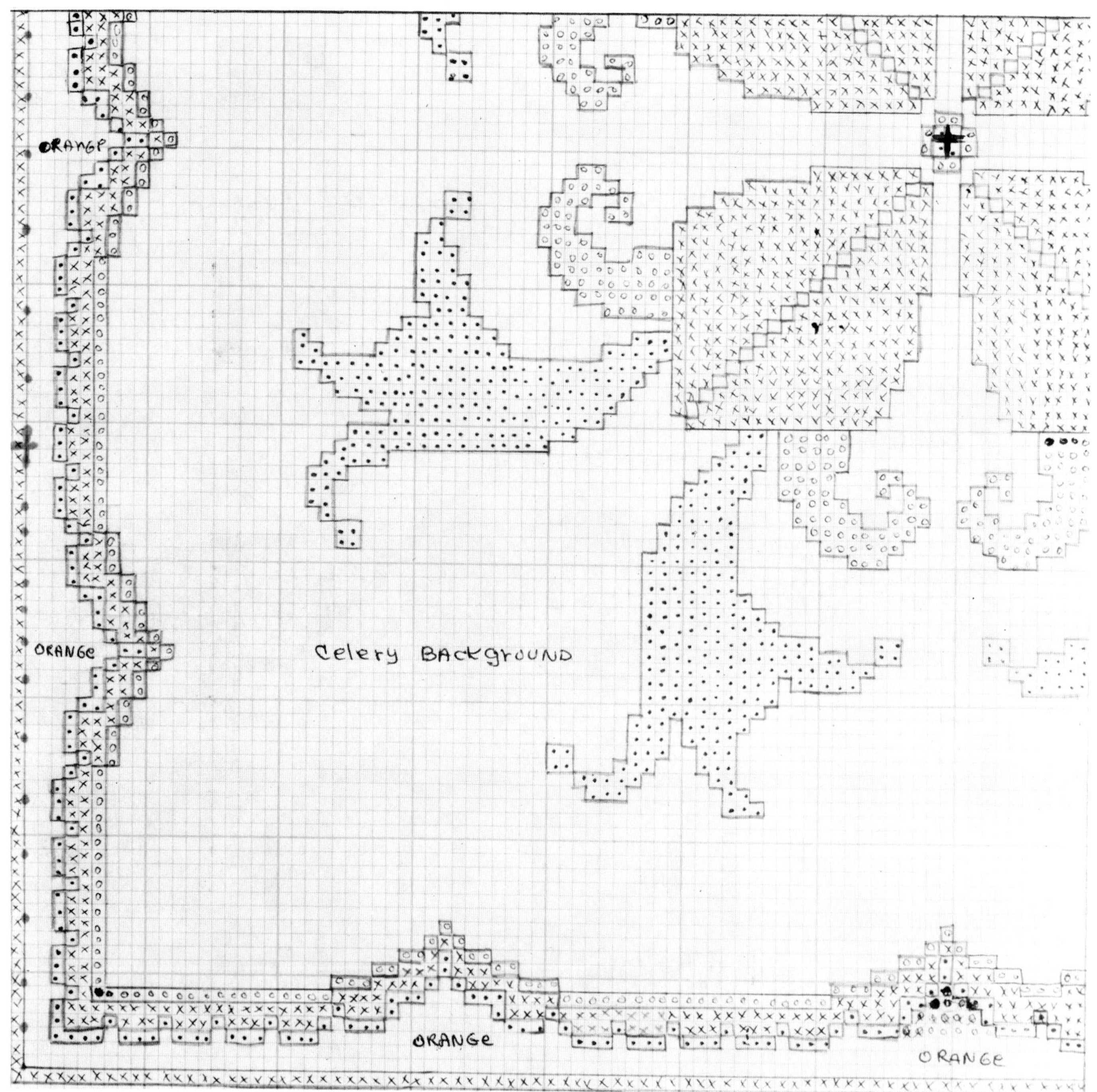

COLORS:

- ⊡ **Bright Yellow**
- ☒ **Turquoise Blue**
- ⊙ **Orange**

Celery background

"PLUMES"

1. Start with the center four yellow stitches.
2. Orange stitches around yellow center.
3. Outline blue starting from the center. Outline each unit, then fill in with the turquoise.
4. Outline the orange Plumes first, then fill in.
5. Outline the yellow Plumes, then fill in.
6. Start the orange border from the center, then working towards the corners.
7. Blue next.
8. Yellow last.
9. Blue edge over one, two, or three threads.
10. Work the orange in between the borders.
11. Do the background in celery.

SIZE: 14″x 14″

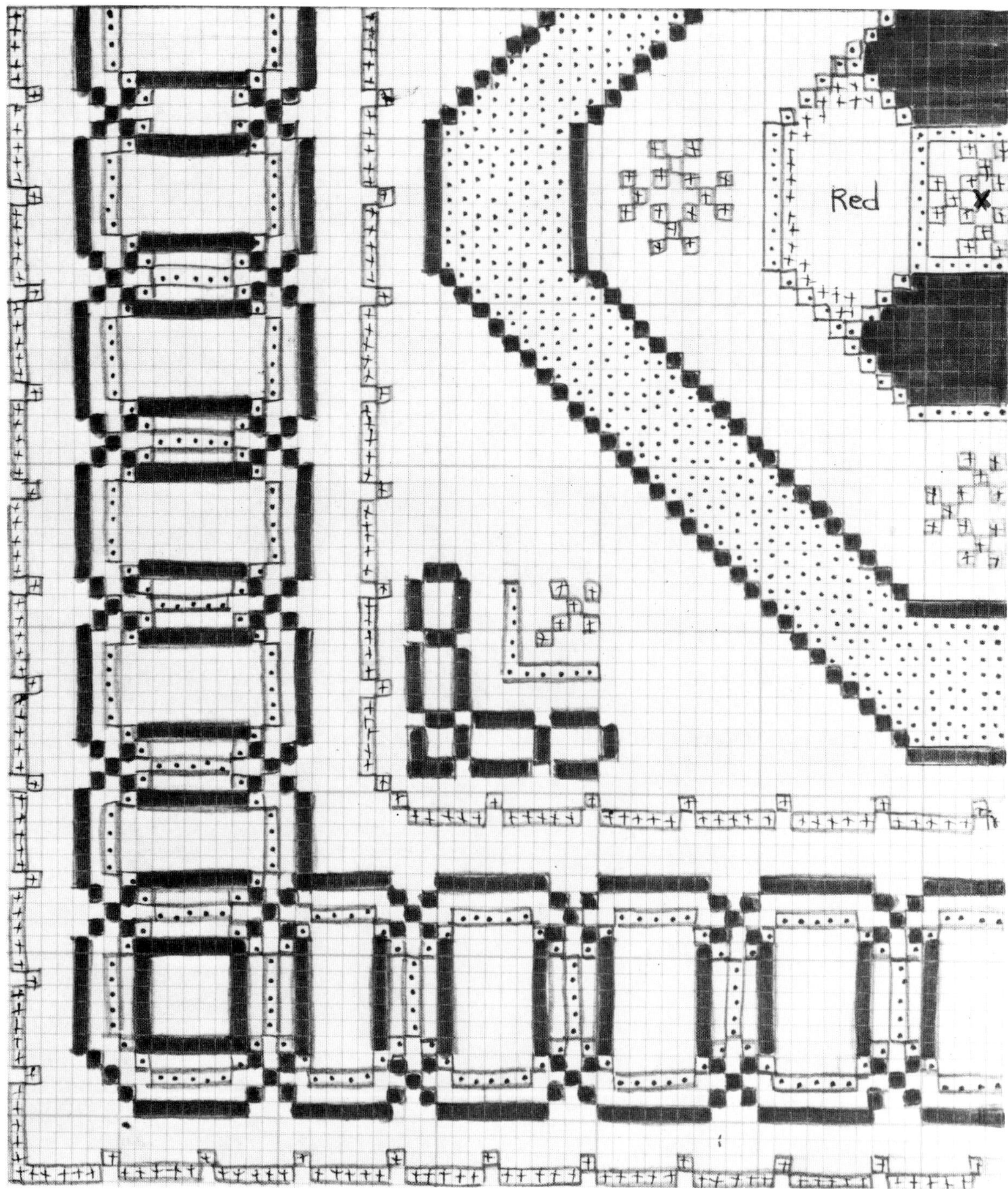

COLORS:

- Turquoise Blue
- Bright Yellow
- Fire Red

White background

1. Begin with the center red stitches.
2. Outline the pattern in yellow.
3. Fill in yellow outline in red.
4. Do both blue outlines, starting in the center.
5. Now fill in outline in yellow.
6. Do red stitches in between the two patterns.
7. Begin your red border on your center thread.
8. Work the blue corner motif, then the red.
9. Complete your red border on the edge before you start the pattern on the border. It will be easier to both count stitches and confine your work.
10. Start with the top blue outline, beginning in the center doing the bars and the three stitches first.
11. Now you can do the rest of the blue outline, working in a loop and circle rhythm.
12. Follow the same rhythm with the red outline. Top first, then the bottom.
13. White background can now be done.

SIZE: 12″x 12″

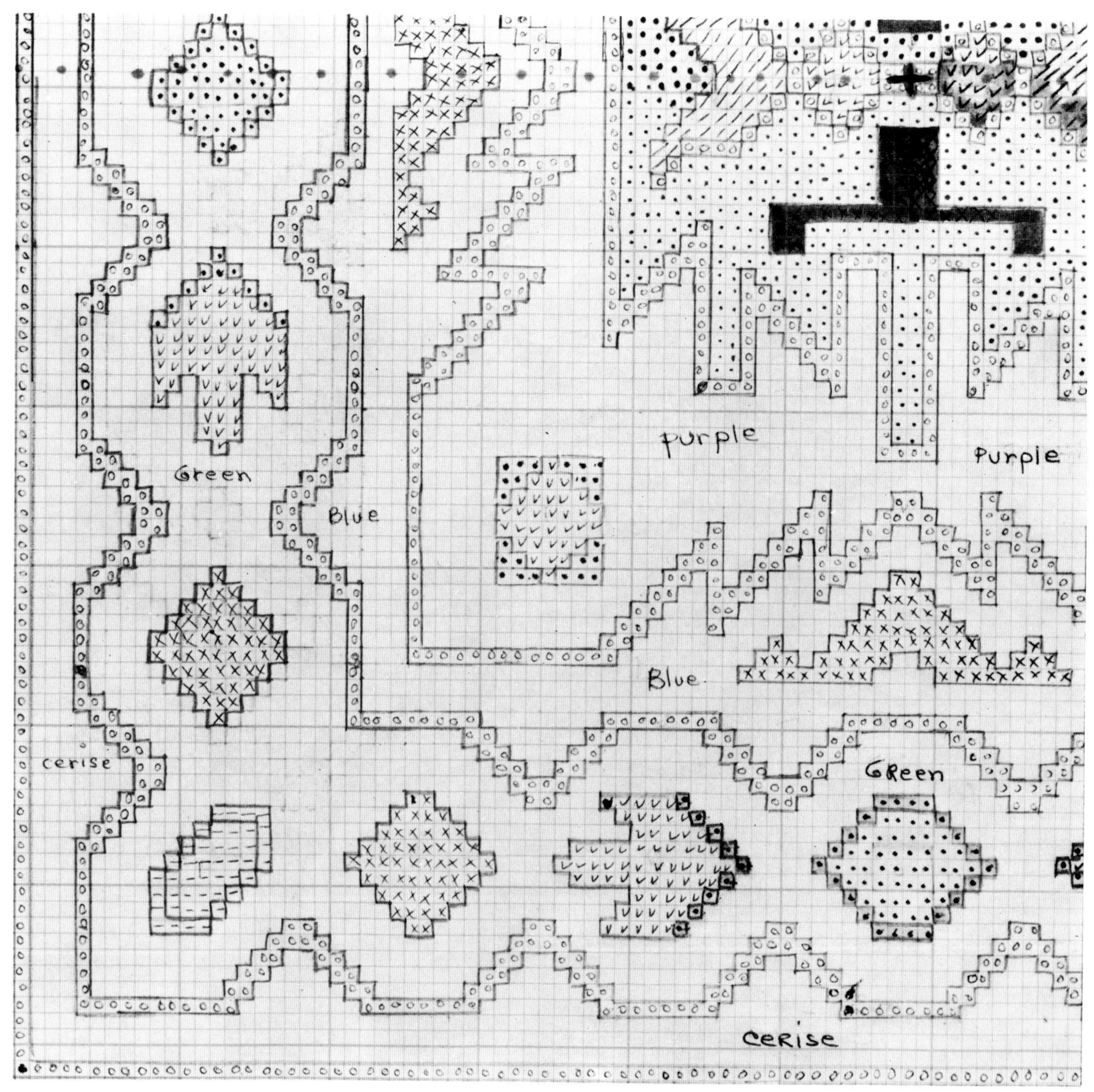

COLORS:

- Lemon Yellow
- Cerise
- Purple
- Turquoise Blue
- White

"INCA"

1. Start with the eight white stitches in the center.
2. Continue the white into the outline, doing the inside first, then the outside outline.
3. Fill in the pattern with the proper colors as indicated on the graph.
4. Do all your white outlines first, then fill in with the designs.
5. After all the patterns have been worked, then you can do the background starting with the yellow in the middle, then the purple, the blue the green, and finally the cerise.
6. This is one of the easiest patterns. Once the outline is out of the way, the rest is a breeze.

SIZE: 12″x 12½″

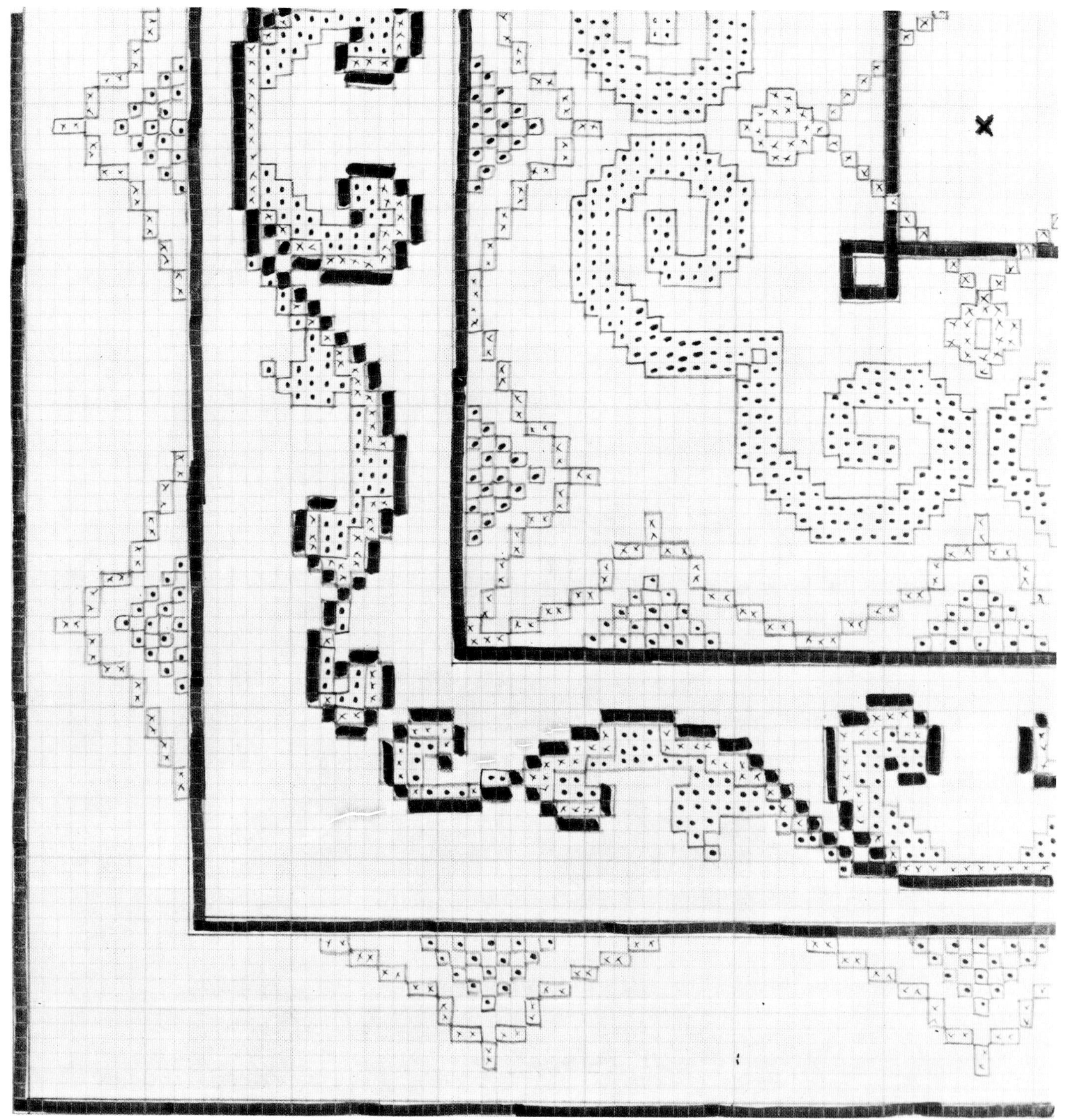

COLORS:

■ **Black**
☒ **Orange**
⊡ **Yellow**

White background

"YANGTZE SWIRLS"

1. You begin with the black square in the center.
2. Now you do the orange diamond around the black square.
3. Outline the yellow scroll first starting with the top row. Begin in the center and work your way to the other center. Do each row, one by one.
4. The black border before you work the rest of the middle.
5. Start the orange outline on the center thread, use the black border as a guide.
6. Do the center border, in black.
7. Now the last border, in black.
8. Begin your black outline on the center thread, count carefully.
9. Orange next.
10. Now the yellow.
11. On your last border pattern, begin with the yellow, then the orange.
12. The background, using the white yarn.

SIZE: 13″x 13″

COLORS:

- Black
- Plum
- Royal Blue
- Apple Green

Lemon Yellow background

"ISTANBUL"

1. Begin with the black outline in the center of the pattern, starting with the center thread.
2. Now do the plum outline.
3. Fill in with the proper colors, completing the center design.
4. Outline the black bars.
5. Fill in the bars in royal blue.
6. Do the black borders first.
7. Now outline in black the scrolls.
8. Fill in with the plum.
9. The two corner arrows.
10. The black and plum border.
11. Fill in the center in yellow.
12. Outline in black the scrolls.
13. Fill in the scrolls in royal blue.
14. Black and plum border.
15. One row in yellow.
16. One row in black.
17. Do the outside border in apple green.

SIZE: 13″x 13″

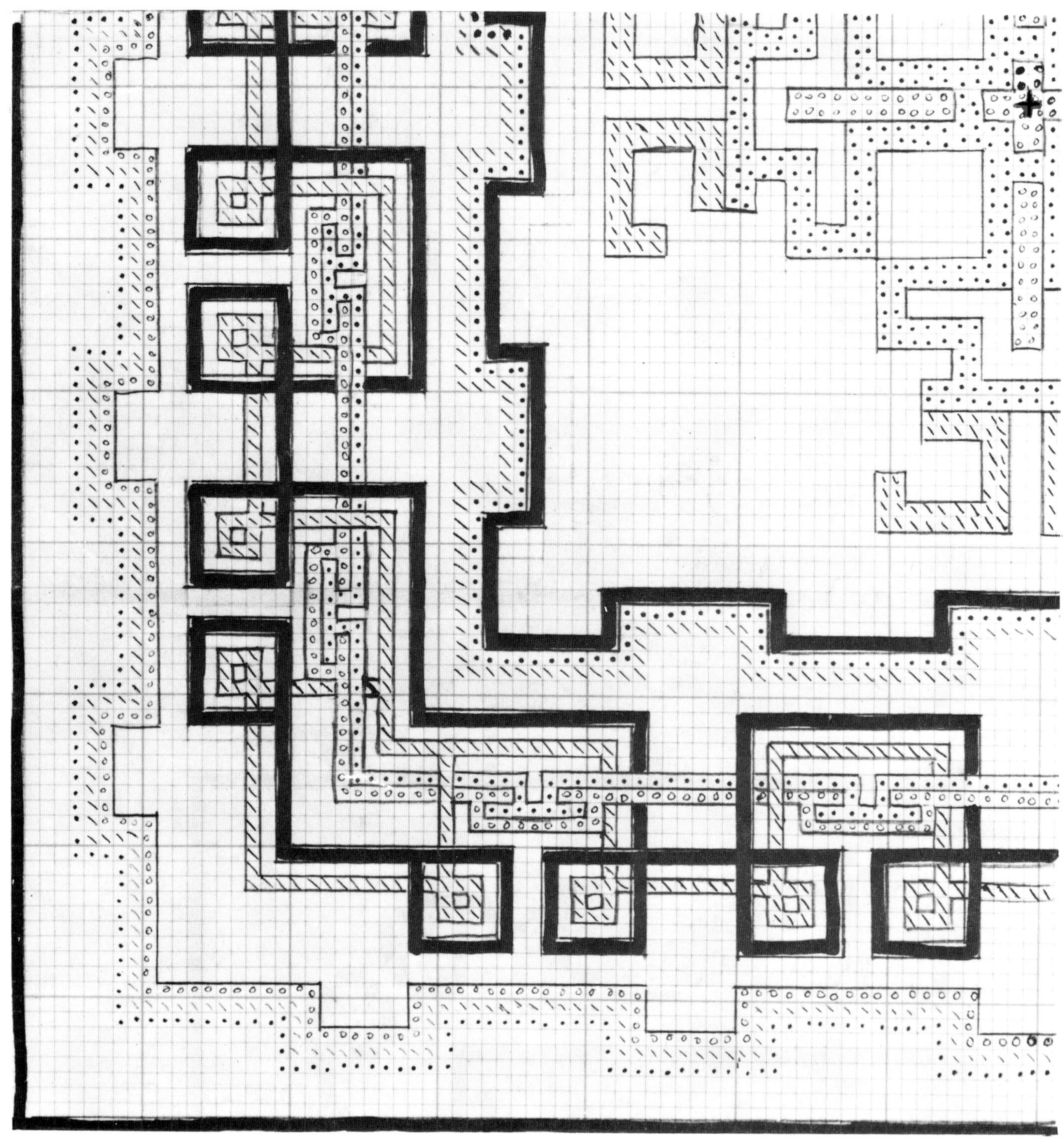

COLORS:

■ **Black**
⊡ **Yellow**
⧅ **Emerald Green**
⊙ **Orange**

White and Green background

"CHINESE KEY"

1. You start with the orange cross in the center.
2. The yellow pattern around the cross.
3. Now the green.
4. The black border first.
5. The yellow border.
6. The green border.
7. Do all the black outlines, counting carefully and referring to the graph as needed.
8. Now the green inside the black.
9. Start with the yellow lines first, then the orange one.
10. Edge the pattern with the black border, working the black over two or three threads.
11. Begin your border design with the orange, working your way down with the green and finally the yellow.
12. White background.

SIZE: 14″x 14″

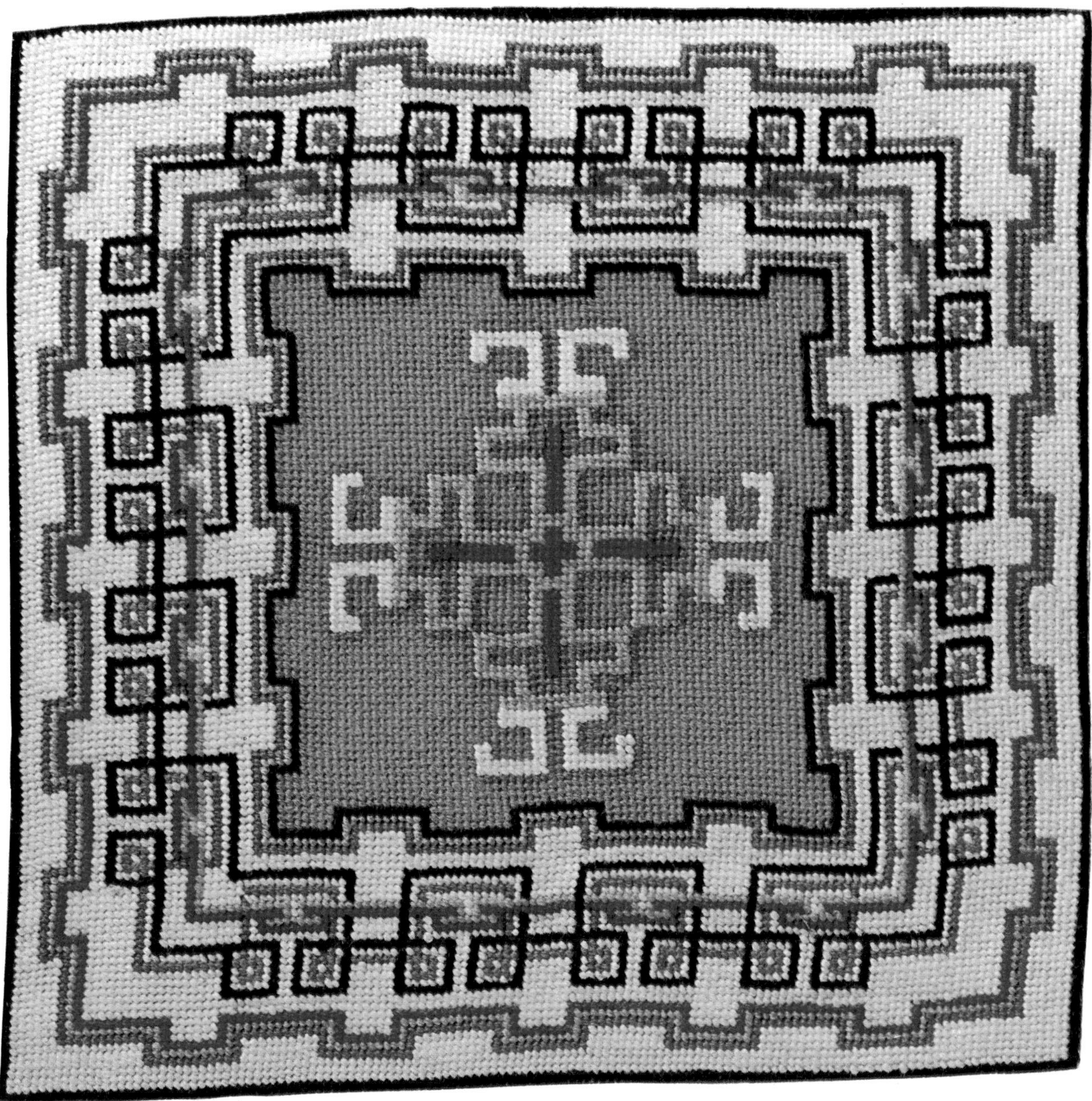

COLORS:

- ■ **Purple**
- ⊡ **Yellow**
- ☒ **Lime Green**
- ⊙ **Dark Green**
- ⧄ **Orange**
- ⊟ **White**

Orange and White backgrounds

"FLEUR-DE-LIS"

1. Start with the orange center.
2. Do the lime green outline.
3. Now the purple inside the outline.
4. Begin your dark green outline in the center.
5. Do all the lime green outlines in the middle design.
6. Follow through with the purple.
7. Now the yellow.
8. Fill the small purple square that connects the dark green loops, in orange.
9. Purple center border.
10. Follow the same method in the last border design, as was used above.
11. Purple edge, doing the two purple first, then filling in with the lime green, dark green, orange and white.
12. Do the middle background in white.
13. The bottom background in orange.

SIZE: 16″ x 16″

"GARDEN CIRCULAR"

1. Begin your pattern with the four black stitches in the center of the graph, where the red X is.
2. The orange pattern around the black.
3. The chartreuse outline.
4. Yellow outline.
5. The black outline underneath the yellow outline.
6. Start your border design with the yellow motif right in the center of your canvas.
7. The yellow squares in between the yellow motifs.
8. The orange design starting from in between the yellow squares.

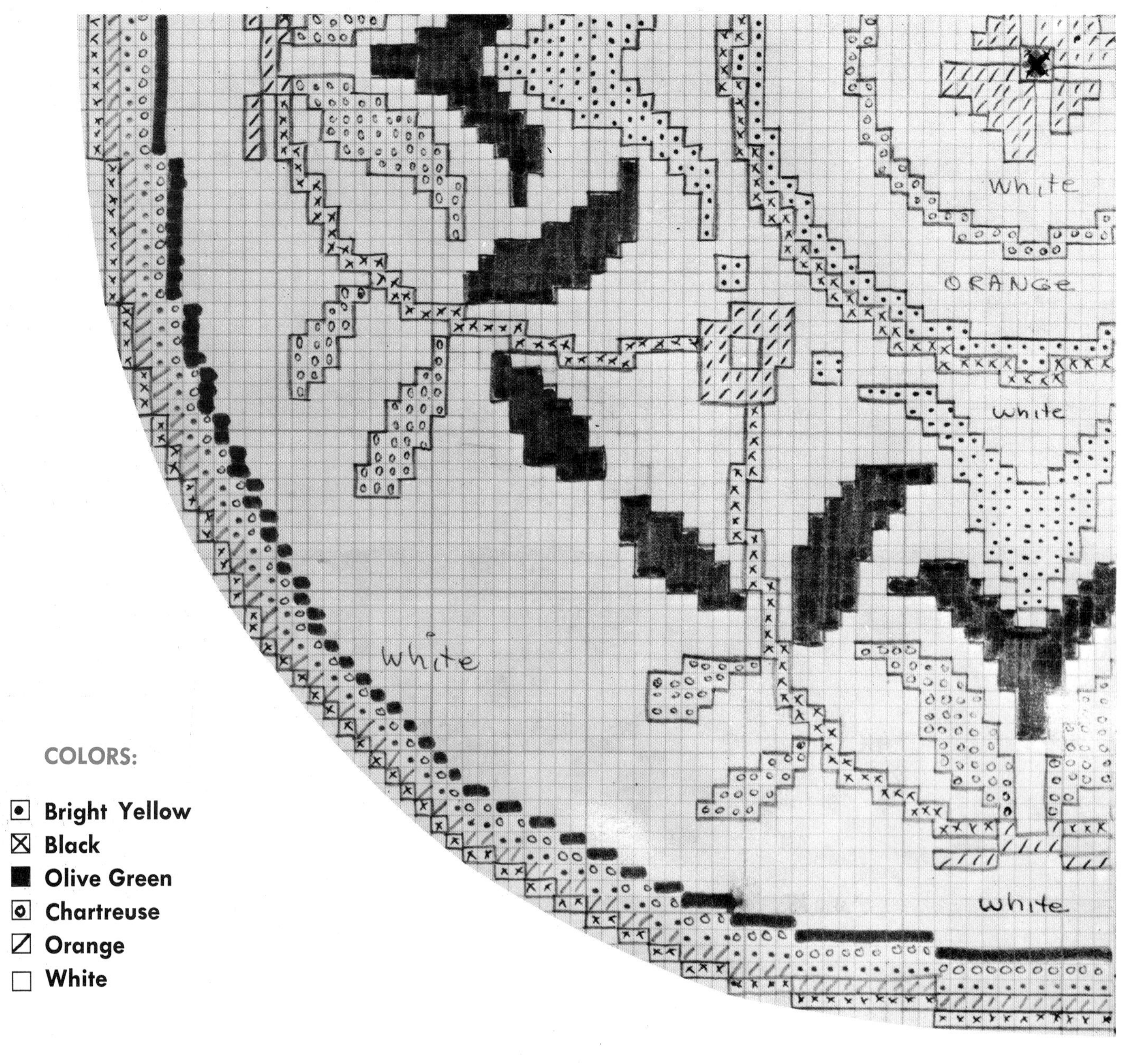

COLORS:

- ⊡ **Bright Yellow**
- ☒ **Black**
- ■ **Olive Green**
- ◙ **Chartreuse**
- ⧄ **Orange**
- □ **White**

9. Now do the black that branches out from the orange design.
10. The orange that is a continuation of the black and connects the black in the center of canvas.
11. The olive green leaves under the worked yellow motif.
12. The chartreuse leaves under the olive green leaves.
13. The olive green leaves branching out from the black outline.
14. Chartreuse leaves branching out from the black outline.
15. A single row of each of the following colors, in the order given: olive, chartreuse, yellow, and orange.
16. Complete the border with three rows of black worked row by row, to give a corded look.
17. The center background is worked in white.
18. The background in between the chartreuse and yellow is done in orange.
19. The final background on the border is done in white.

SIZE: 12″ x 12″ ROUND

COLORS:

■ Black
▨ White
⊡ Chocolate Brown

Gold background

"SNOW FLAKE"

1. You start with the white box in the center.
2. Do all the black outlines in the center.
3. Then all the white outlines, including the middle border.
4. Now do the brown.
5. Begin the border with the four center motifs, saving the corner motifs for later.
6. Outline all the black designs first, then fill in with the black.
7. Now you can do the corner motifs.
8. Do the white border.
9. Black border over two or three threads.
10. For the background select a warm, orangey gold.

SIZE: 15″x 15″

TOP

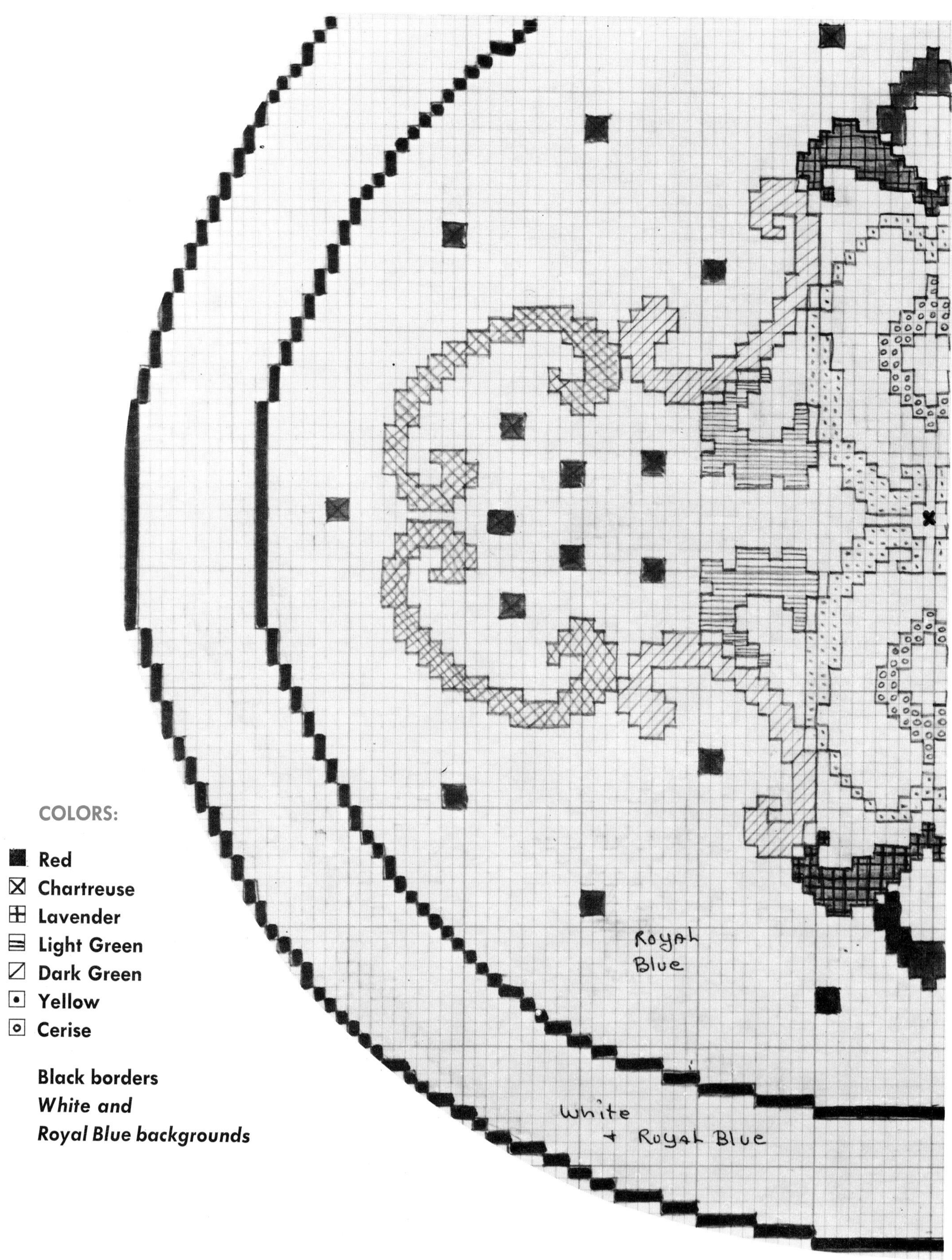
Royal Blue
White + Royal Blue
COLORS:
Red
Chartreuse
Lavender
Light Green
Dark Green
Yellow
Cerise
Black borders
White and
Royal Blue backgrounds

"PAGODA"

1. You begin with the yellow, starting from the center and working your way around to the other center.
2. The cerise inside the yellow outline.
3. Now the lavender.
4. Do the red underneath the lavender, and save the red boxes for later.
5. Follow through with the dark green, light green and chartreuse. In that order.
6. Do the two black border outlines. Doing the last one in two or three separate rows for a heavier border.
7. Now you can do the red boxes. You can do them in the Double Cross stitch for a raised effect.
8. Fill in the center background in royal blue.
9. Do the outside border in royal blue and white Mosaic stitch done diagonally.
10. This is a great pattern to use if you have just a few strands of many colors left over. Combine them together to see if they blend well.

SIZE: 12″x 14″ ROUND

TOP

COLORS:

■ Dark Blue
⊡ Medium Blue
● Light Blue
⧄ White

"BLUE DELFT"

1. Start the pattern with the ten dark blue stitches in the center of the graph, in the center of your canvas.
2. Do the medium blue outline around the ten stitches.
3. Fill inside the finished outline in a lighter blue.
4. Now the dark blue outline. Save the white center for later.
5. Medium blue design around the blue outline.
6. Fill in worked area with your lighter blue.
7. Begin your middle outline in dark blue, starting in the center of your canvas and working your way around. Do one line at a time.
8. Work the medium blue inside the darker outline.
9. Complete this design.
10. Do the outer border starting with the dark blue pattern. Begin with the center pattern, then working the corners.
11. The medium blue inside and outside the border.
12. Complete the design.
13. Do the dark border on the edge, two rows, one at a time.
14. The medium border, also two rows, one at a time.
15. The center background in white.
16. The middle background in white.
17. The next to the last, in light blue.
18. The edge border in white.

SIZE: 13″x 15″

COLORS:

- ⊡ Bright Red
- B ■ Black
- ⊙ Bright Yellow
- ⊠ Emerald Green

"TIBET"

1. Start with the green center.
2. Do the yellow around the green.
3. Do the red outline.
4. Now the black outline.
5. Fill in the center pattern in green.
6. Fill in the black design in red.
7. Red border.
8. Black border.
9. Fill in with green in between the inside black and the red border.
10. Do the yellow in between the black and red border.
11. Red border.
12. The yellow above this border.
13. The last red border.
14. Fill in the design starting with the yellow, then the red, etc.
15. This background gets filled in with black.
16. Black border.
17. Red border.
18. Green border.
19. Fill in the rest of pattern in yellow.

SIZE: 14″x 14″

COLORS:

- ⊡ **Orange**
- ☐ **Deep Turquoise Blue**
- ■ **Black**

White background

"PATCHWORK"

1. Begin your pattern with the orange center design.
2. Outline first, then fill in.
3. Blue arrows. Follow this rhythm in working. Section by section.
4. Black and white center border.
5. Blue pattern top and bottom of worked design.
6. Orange corners.
7. Black and white borders all around.
8. Blue middle design that's left to work.
9. White background.

SIZE: 12½″x 12½″

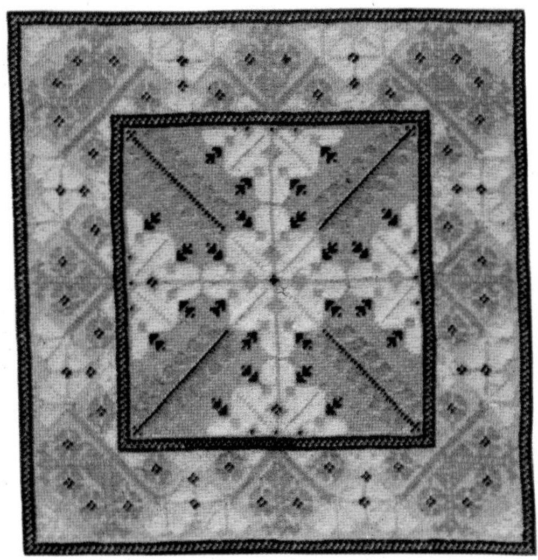

Intermediate Designs

TOP

COLORS:

- Black
- Yellow
- Dark Green
- White
- Orange
- Royal Blue
- Lime Green

"SERAPE"

1. You begin the pattern with the yellow center.
2. Outline the center in white.
3. Do all the black outlining in the middle section.
4. Next do all the dark green inside this area.
5. Complete all the patterns.
6. Fill in the background in orange.
7. Lime green border.
8. Start the border design with the white outline and going from there to complete the pattern.
9. Edge the border, first with the black, then yellow, orange, dark green, lime green, white and finally the black again. Do one row of each color.

SIZE: 10″x 14″

COLORS:

- ■ Navy
- ⊡ Gold
- ⊙ Emerald Green
- ⧄ Fire Red

"OMAR KHAYYAM"

1. Outline entire middle section in gold.
2. Fill in the outline in navy.
3. Outline in gold the beginning of your outside border.
4. Do the navy design underneath the gold outline.
5. Fill in with the green inside the navy pattern.
6. Now do the red background in the center section that has been worked.
7. Outline the stars in navy.
8. Complete the inside of stars.
9. Work the lower navy design, using the same method used in number four.
10. Fill in around the stars in gold.
11. Do the navy and gold border, three rows separately.
12. Fill in with the red inside the border.

SIZE: 16″x 16″

TOP

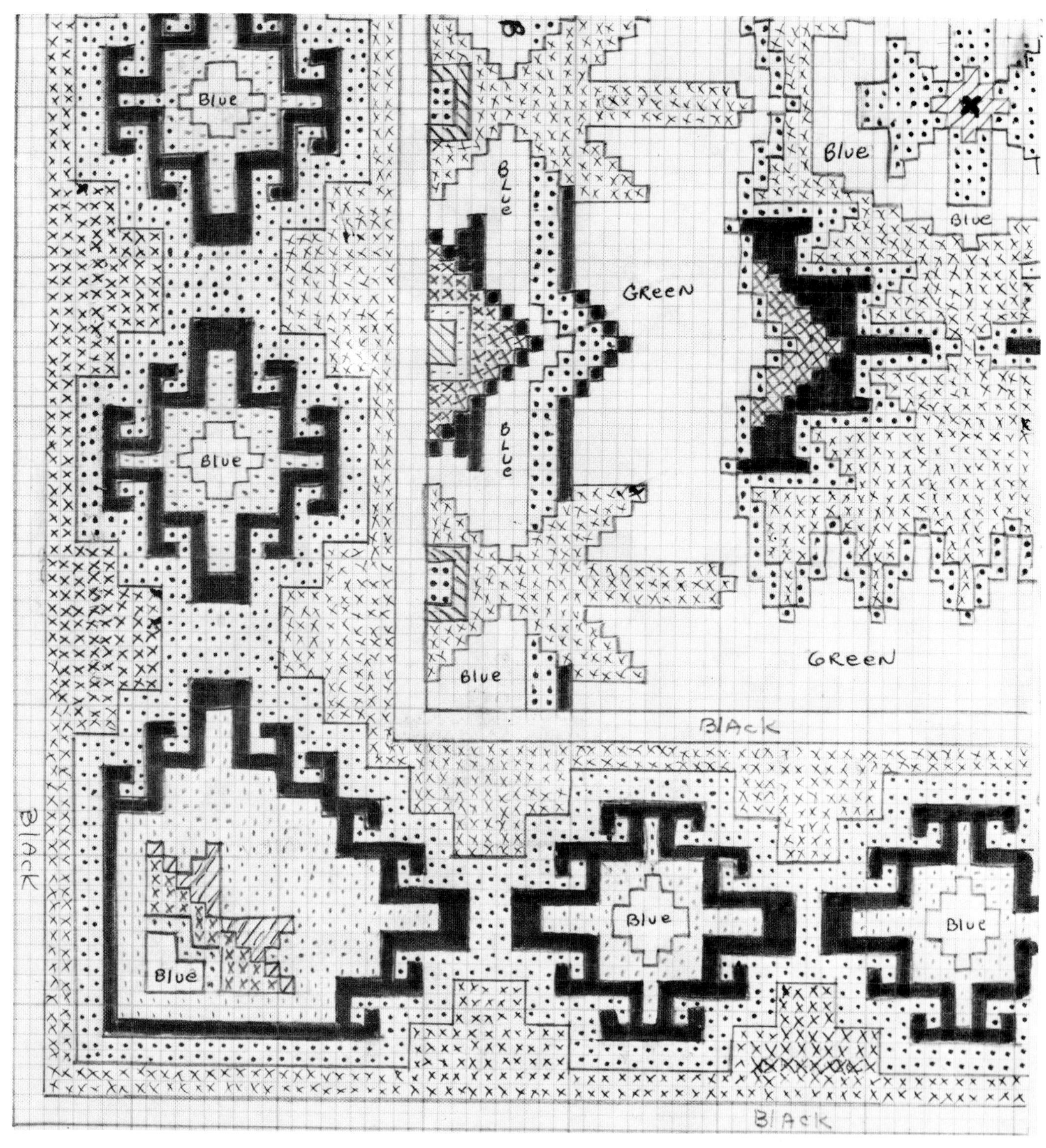

COLORS:

- ⊡ **Yellow**
- ◿ **Green**
- ■ **Purple**
- ⊠ **Orange**
- 🅱 **Blue**

Black borders

"XOCHIMILCO"

1. Make the center green cross first.
2. Outline that with the yellow, then fill in.
3. Do the yellow outlines, then fill in with the orange, then the purple.
4. Work two rows of black for the border in the middle.
5. Do the orange, then the purple.
6. Complete the design including the green and blue background.
7. Begin the border design with the purple motifs.
8. Then the yellow, outlining first.
9. The blue centers.
10. The corner designs.
11. Fill in with yellow.
12. Two single rows of black for the border.
13. Finish the border in orange.

SIZE: 14″x 14″

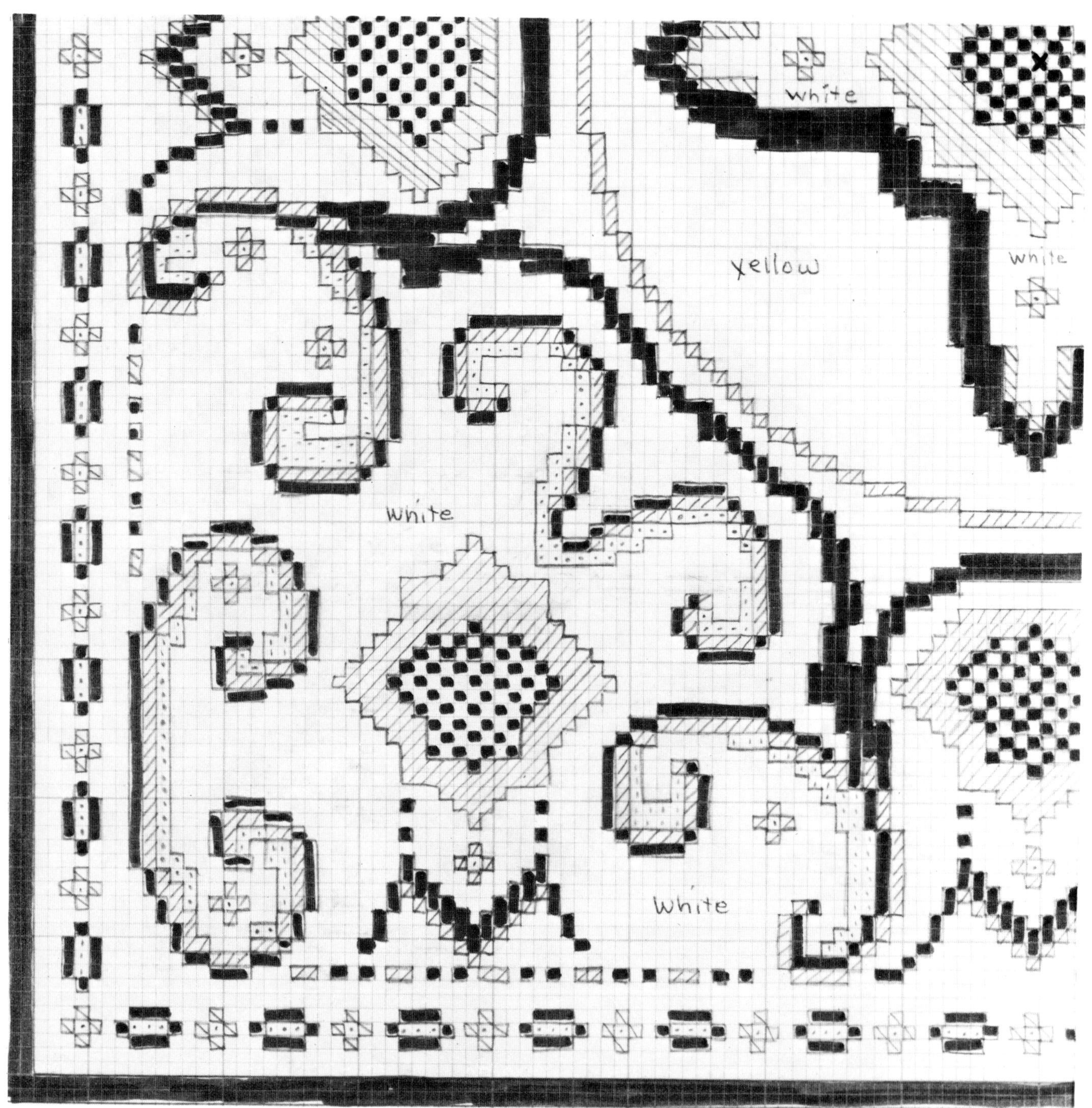

COLORS:

- ■ **Green**
- ⊡ **Yellow**
- ⧄ **Coral**

White background

"RENAISSANCE"

1. Begin the pattern with the green center.
2. Outline the center in coral and fill in.
3. Work the green, a row at a time.
4. Finish the coral.
5. Dot each coral cross in yellow.
6. Complete the background in the worked area in white.
7. Do the coral circle.
8. Do all the green outlining, including the border.
9. Complete the swirls in coral and yellow.
10. The coral diamonds.
11. Finish all the other details.
12. Do the yellow background inside the coral circle.
13. The rest of the background is in white.

SIZE: 15″x15″

TOP

COLORS:

- Orange
- Red
- Dark Green
- Light Green
- Dark Blue
- Light Blue
- Yellow

White background

"FIESTA"

1. Begin with the two dark green centers.
2. Fill in center in light green.
3. Do the orange outlines.
4. Now the red outlines.
5. Fill in the outlines.
6. Dark green leaves and the middle border.
7. Fill in leaves in light green.
8. Work the flowers first, the center ones then the corners.
9. Leaves. The dark green first, then the light green.
10. Dark green border, do three separate rows.
11. Finish the pattern.
12. White background.

SIZE: 14½"x14½" ROUND

COLORS:

- ☒ **Hot Pink**
- ⊡ **Red**
- ☑ ■ **Light Green**
- ⊡ **Dark Green**
- ◪ **Burgundy**

White background

"PSYCHEDELIC"

1. Start the design with the light green stem that branches out from the center.
2. Do the burgundy outline.
3. Fill in center in hot pink.
4. Do all the dark green outlines, counting carefully and checking with the graph to avoid any errors.
5. Fill the outline with the light green.
6. Complete the centers of the green motif, first with the red, then with the burgundy.
7. Now begin the middle motif, first with the red starting from the tip of the plumes.
8. Next do the hot pink.
9. The light green cross.
10. Finally the burgundy.
11. Dark green border, two or three single rows.
12. Do the background in white.

SIZE: 14″x 14″

TOP

COLORS:

- ⊞ **Light Gold**
- ☒ **Green**
- ■ **Black**
- ⊡ **Dark Gold**
- ◙ **Bright Red**

"MANCHU"

1. Mark the top of your canvas with TOP.
2. Begin your pattern with the center red outline.
3. Do the left and right red outline.
4. Now when working the rest of the pattern make sure to fill in with the proper design as both sides are different. That's the purpose for marking the top of your design. You can now refer to the graph without confusion.
5. Once you have completed the work around the four middle motifs, begin the black outline, starting from the center of the pattern and working out towards the corners.
6. Complete the inside of the black outlines.
7. Do the two black borders. The edge border over three threads.
8. Start the border design with the black outline, starting in the center and working out to the corners.
9. Next do the light gold with the dark gold centers.
10. Do the dark gold outline and complete the pattern.
11. The background in the center is in red.
12. The border in green.
13. Work light gold closest to the edge.
14. Select your golds from the same family.

SIZE: 14″x 15″

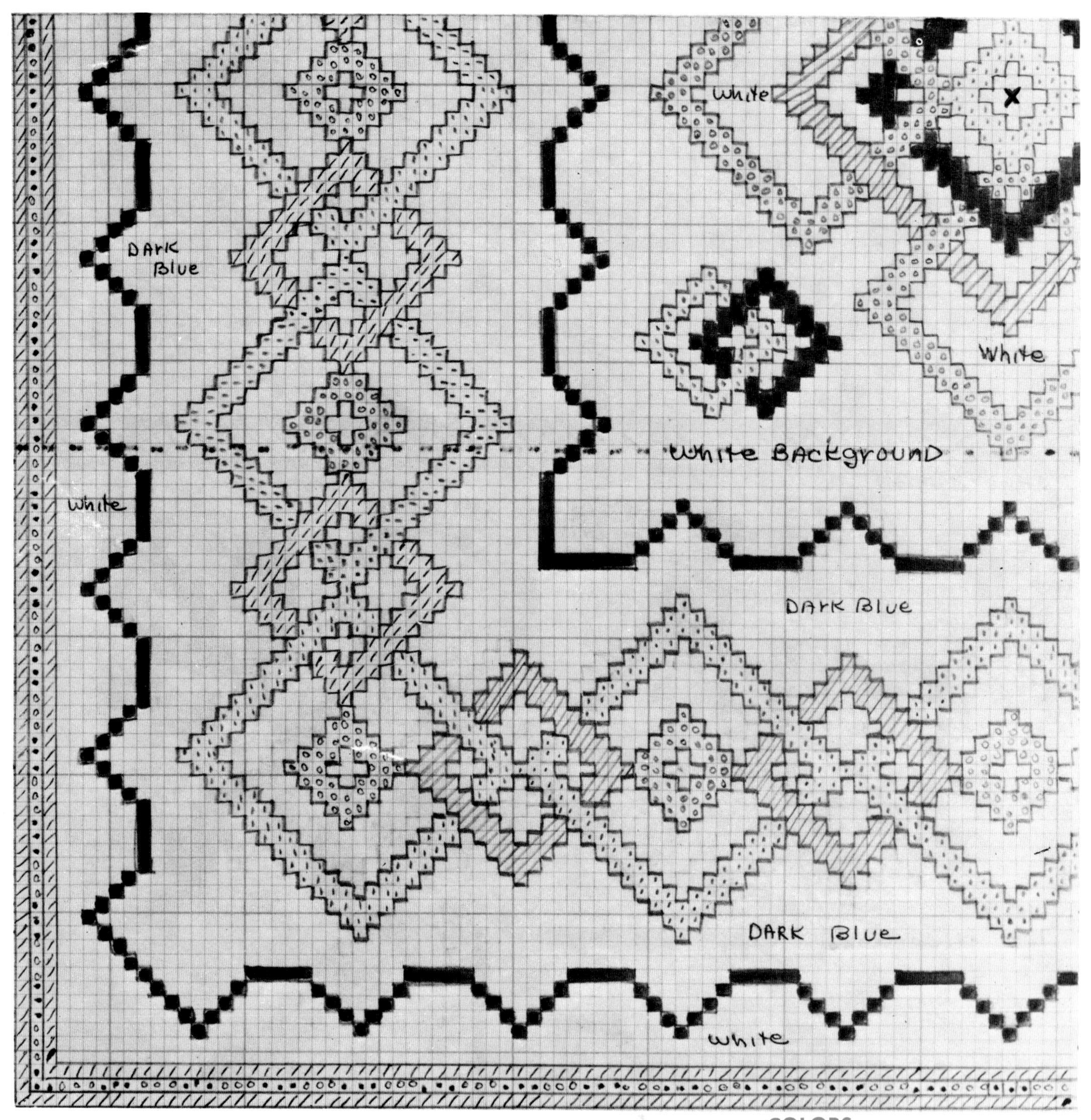

COLORS:

- ■ Salmon
- ⊙ Powder Blue
- ⧄ Bright Green
- ⊡ Strong Yellow

Darker Blue and White backgrounds

"ZIG-ZAG

1. Begin the pattern with the yellow center.
2. Continue the yellow pattern in the powder blue.
3. Now do the salmon in the center.
4. Complete the design with the green.
5. Do the middle border in salmon.
6. Finish the design with the corner motif.
7. Start the border design with the yellow, using the salmon border as a guide.
8. Do the powder blue centers.
9. Connect the powder blue centers to the green design.
10. Salmon border.
11. Outer border, first green, then powder blue, then green again.
12. The entire center inside the salmon outline is done in a white background.
13. The border inside the two salmon outlines is done in a darker blue.
14. The edge that remains is done in white.
15. Combine your colors together before starting. Select the blues that complements the other colors. Choose either orange or salmon, whichever is needed to go with the darker blue.

SIZE: 14½"x14½"

COLORS:

- ⊡ **Gold**
- ■ **Brown**
- ◿ **Medium Blue**

Light Blue and Melon backgrounds

"ILLUSION"

1. Start with the four brown stitches in the center.
2. Begin the gold outline from the center, then filling in.
3. Do the center border in light blue and brown.
4. Do the brown center of the feather like pattern.
5. Now do the medium blue outline, then fill it in.
6. Complete center pattern with the brown designs.
7. Do the edge border in light blue and brown.
8. Begin the outer border with the medium blue center pattern. Corner for last.
9. Do all the small gold designs closest to the middle blue and brown border.
10. Now the medium blue flowers with the brown centers.
11. Now you can work the corner, using the worked designs as a guide.
12. Complete all details.
13. Center background in melon.
14. Border background in light blue.

SIZE: 17″x 17″

COLORS:

- ☒ Red
- ⊡ Yellow
- ◿ Hot Pink
- ⊟ Orange
- ■ Black
- □ White
- G ⊡ Emerald Green

"SHAH BORDER"

1. Begin the center design with the black outline, starting with the center.
2. Complete the entire black outline, then fill in with the proper colors.
3. Black center border.
4. Do all the black zig-zag outlining, including the corners.
5. Now do the yellow borders, top and bottom.
6. You can start filling in the zig-zags, row by row. Starting with the color closest to the black.
7. White border, two separate rows.
8. Black border, also two separate rows.
9. White background in the middle section.
10. Green in between the zig-zags.
11. Yellow inside black corners.
12. The rest of the background in white.

SIZE: 15″x 15″

COLORS:

- ■ Black
- ⊡ Yellow
- □ White
- ☒ Royal Blue
- ⊙ Orange
- ⊞ Green
- ⧄ Plum

"PERSIAN CARPET"

1. Do the complete Black Star outline, starting in the center.
2. Outline in white where shown.
3. Fill in pattern with selected colors.
4. Do the two black borders.
5. Start the middle border with the royal blue zig-zag pattern.
6. Follow the blue zig-zag with the yellow. The same order of color applies for the top as for the bottom zig-zag. Complete design.
7. Do the large zig-zag black outline on the bottom border.
8. Follow through with two rows of black for the edge.
9. Do the rest of the black outlines.
10. Complete the pattern by following a similar rhythm that was established with the above border. Doing row by row.
11. Fill in your center background in white.

SIZE: 12″x 12″

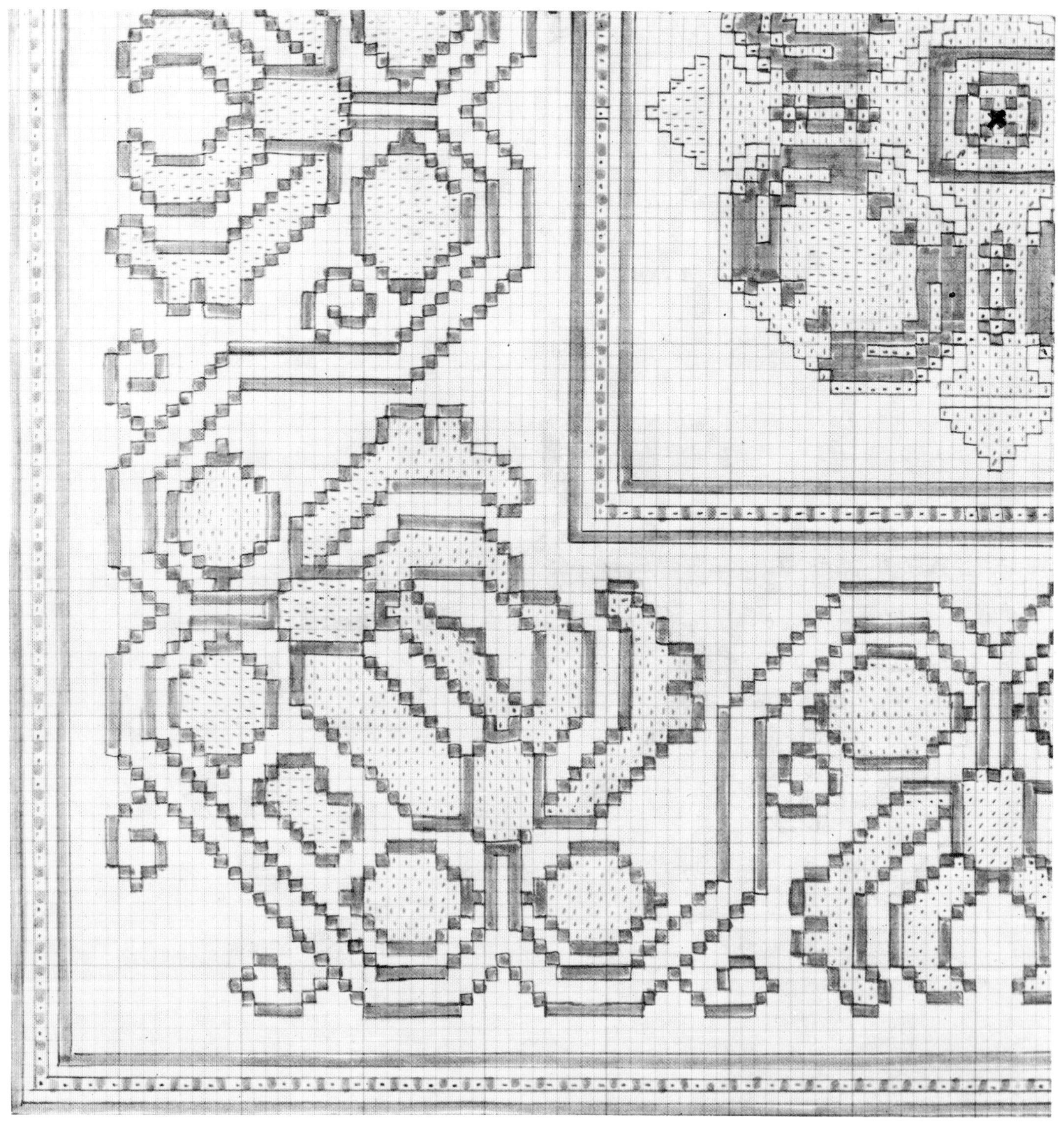

COLORS:

- ⊡ Red
- ■ Bright Yellow

Black background

"CHUNGKING"

1. Begin the design with the yellow center.
2. Make the yellow square around the center.
3. Do the other yellow patterns.
4. Outline in red the entire center. Then fill in.
5. Yellow border.
6. Black border.
7. Red and yellow border.
8. Black border.
9. Yellow border.
10. Fill in center background in black.
11. Outline entire yellow design.
12. Fill in where specified in red.
13. Yellow border.
14. Black border.
15. Red and yellow border.
16. Black border.
17. Yellow border.
18. Complete the background in black.

SIZE: 16″x 16″

TOP

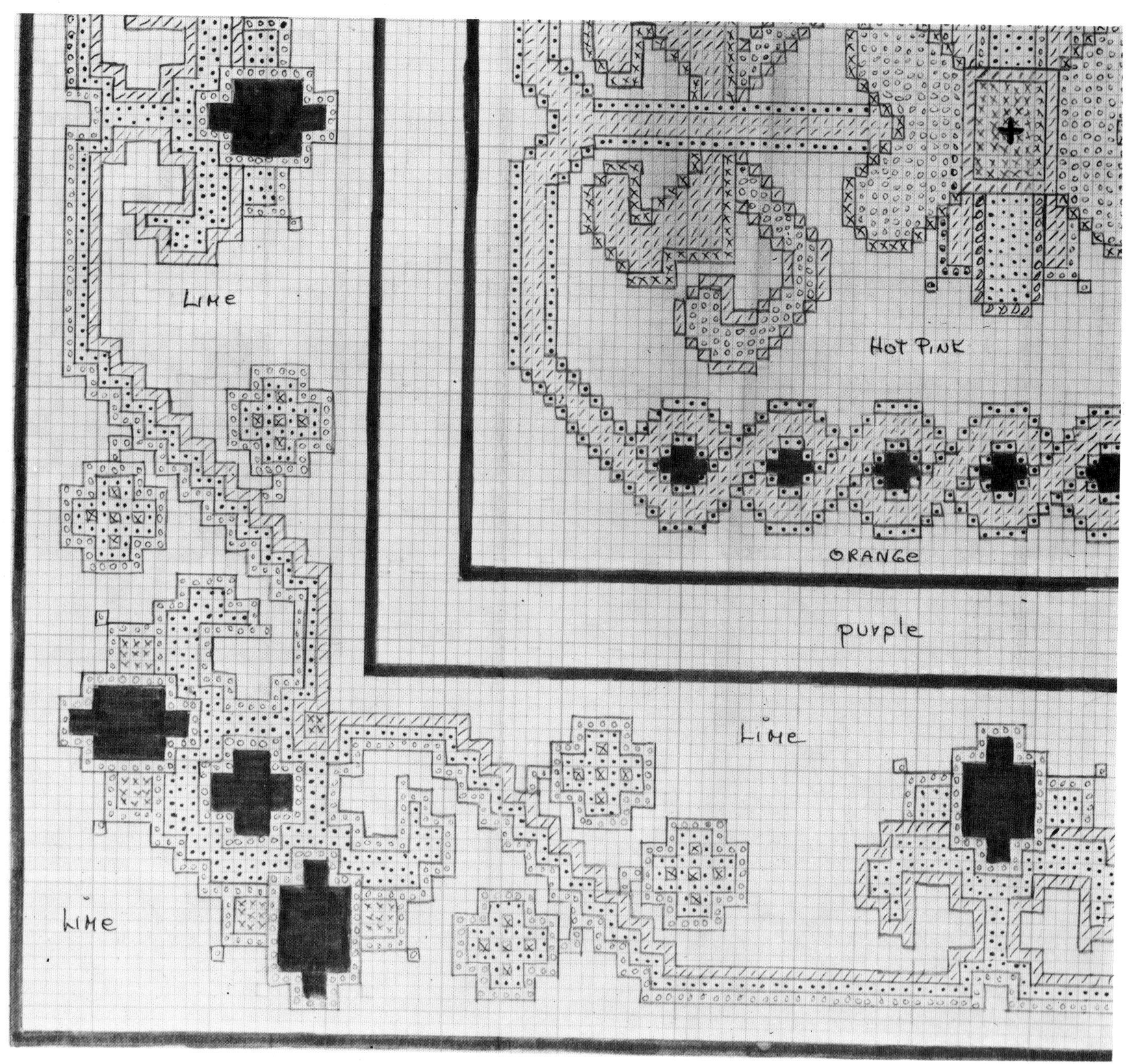

COLORS:

- ■ Hot Pink
- ⊡ Yellow
- ⊠ Lime Green
- ⊙ Orange
- ⧄ Purple

"ACAPULCO"

1. Do the outlining of the center pattern, then filling in with the correct colors.
2. Now do all the yellow outlines in the middle section.
3. Fill in with the purple.
4. Outline the branches inside the yellow.
5. Fill in where needed in this middle section.
6. Do both hot pink borders.
7. Begin the border pattern with the center design, starting with the orange outline.
8. Complete the four designs.
9. Now do the purple outline.
10. The orange outline is next.
11. Do the orange flowers that branch out.
12. Fill in where stated with the yellow, then the hot pink.
13. Hot pink border over three threads.
14. Start doing the background with the hot pink, the orange, the purple, and the lime in that order.

SIZE: 16″x 18″

TOP

"COLLAGE IN BLUE"

1. The X at the top of the pattern marks the center of your design. Match it to the X on your canvas and start from that point.
2. Outline the entire pattern in black.
3. Fill in with proper colors.
4. Black and deep turquoise blue border. Start in the center and work to corners.
5. Pale turquoise blue background.

SIZE: 13″x 20″

COLORS:

- ◩ **White**
- ⊡ **Deep Turquoise Blue**
- ■ **Black outlined**

Pale Turquoise Blue background

TOP

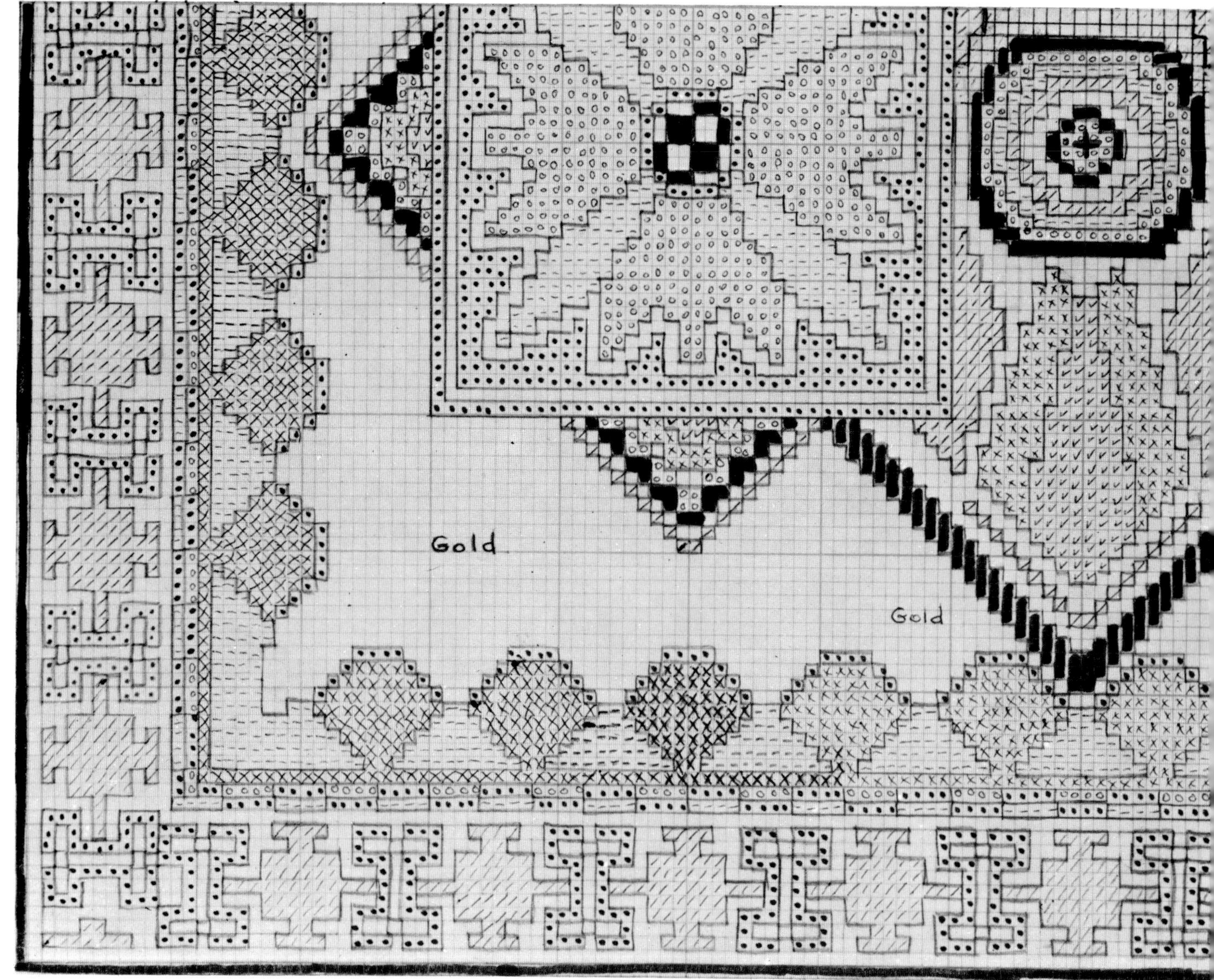

COLORS:

- Rust Orange
- Blue Grey
- Bright Gold
- Beige
- Eggshell
- Black
- Medium Blue
- White

"AZTEC"

1. X marks the center of your pattern. Begin with the gold center.
2. Outline all the black in the center.
3. White around the black.
4. Blue grey around the white.
5. Medium blue around the grey.
6. Now the gold around the blue.
7. Black around worked area.
8. Begin with the orange square, outlining it first.
9. The white border inside the orange square.
10. Do all the orange outlining next to the white border.
11. The gold design.
12. The balance of the design.
13. Do all the black outlining in the center.
14. Work the areas in and around the black outlines.
15. Outline the trees in orange.
16. Medium blue Pyramids.
17. Gold and orange border.
18. Blue grey design on edge.
19. Orange pattern in between the grey.
20. Black border worked over three threads.
21. Finish the area inside the middle design in white.
22. Now gold inside the next area.
23. The border in white.

SIZE: 12″x 16½″

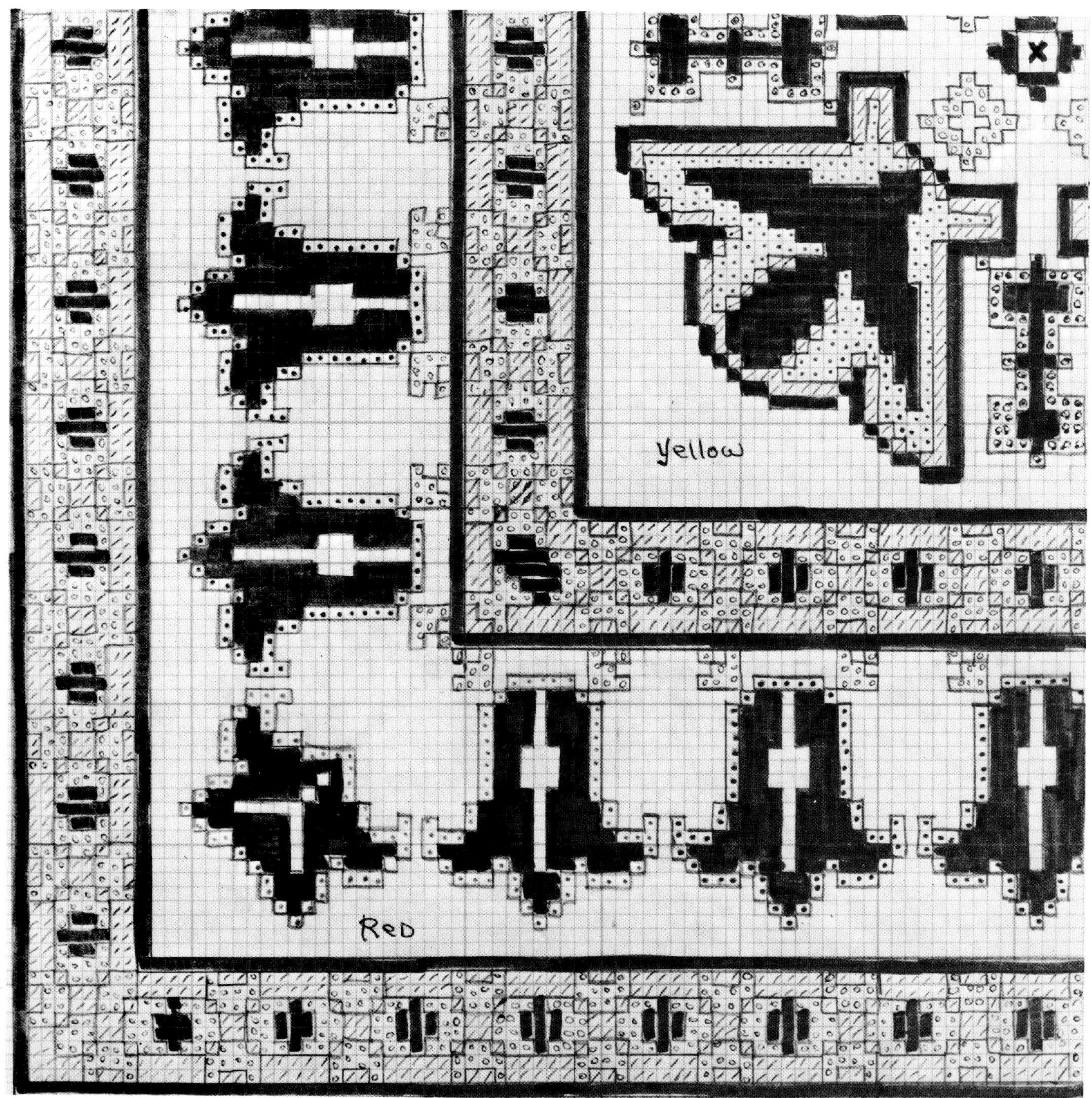

COLORS:

- Black
- Yellow
- Red
- Green

"ORIENTAL BELLS"

1. Start your pattern with the black around the X.
2. Outline all the black in the center.
3. Next do the red.
4. The yellow, the green.
5. The green four motifs around the black center.
6. The center border, outlining the border in black. Do both rows.
7. Black crosses.
8. Red, top and bottom of crosses.
9. Complete border with the green.
10. Outline the bells in yellow.
11. Green arrows.
12. Black inside the yellow outline of the bells.
13. Black border, both rows.
14. Follow the same method used in the center border. Same pattern.
15. Complete the center background in yellow.
16. The background around the bells in red.

SIZE: 15"x15"

Advanced Designs

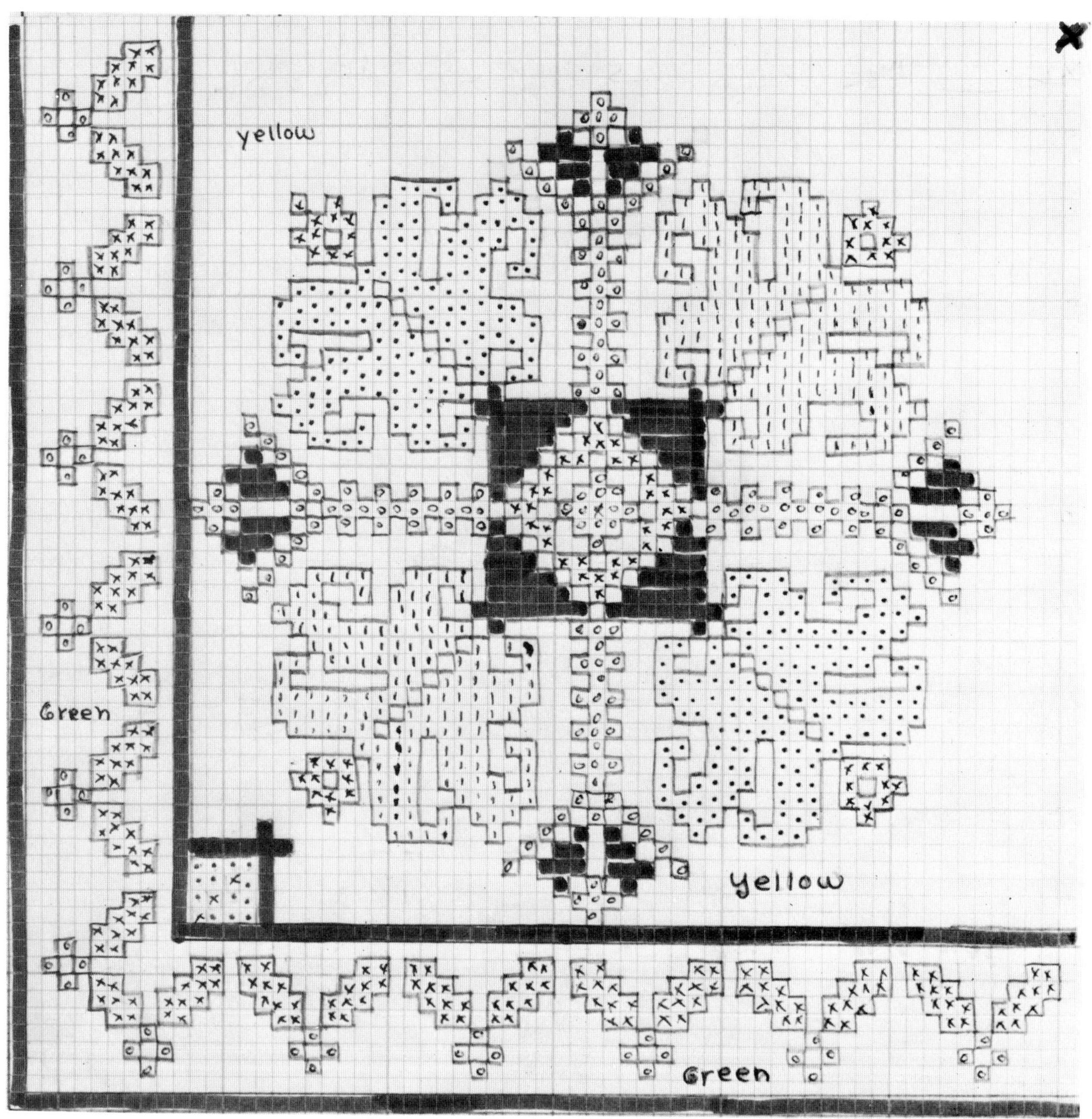

COLORS:

- ◫ **Shocking Blue**
- ⊡ **Cerise**
- ◙ **Light Blue**
- ■ **Royal Blue**
- ☒ **Orange**

Yellow and Bright Green backgrounds

"KALEIDOSCOPE"

1. From the center thread, count down and mark the fifty-third thread from all sides. Use the waterproof pen.
2. Start the pattern from the twenty fifth thread from the marked border. It will be the twenty eighth thread from the center thread.
3. Always begin with the light blue center of the design.
4. Work your way out from this center and completing each section before going on to the other corners.
5. Do the first blue border, in royal including the corner motifs.
6. The edge blue border over two threads.
7. Work the border pattern in orange and light blue.
8. Fill in the center background in yellow.
9. The border background in green.

SIZE: 12½"x 12½"

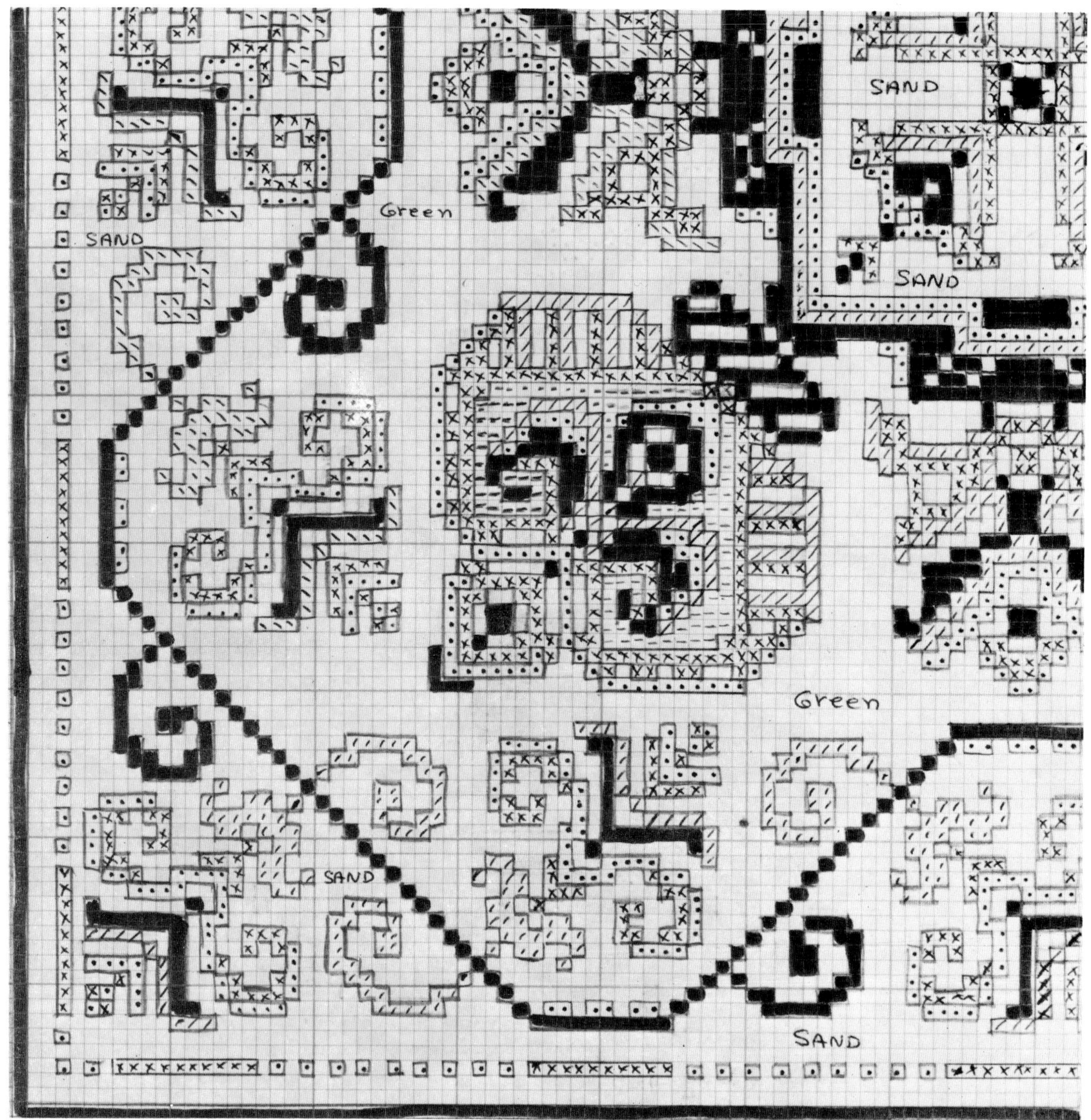

COLORS:

- ■ Medium Brown
- ⊡ Gold Yellow
- ◸ Orange
- ⊠ Medium Blue
- ⊟ Sand

Bright Green and Sand backgrounds

1. Begin the pattern with the brown center eight stitches.
2. Do the blue outline around the brown center.
3. The yellow, brown and blue completing the design.
4. Start the yellow outline from the center and work around to the other centers.
5. The orange underneath yellow outline.
6. Do the brown bars first, then the rest of the brown outline under the yellow and orange outlines.
7. Branch out from the brown outlines, working the center motifs first.
8. The corner motifs, starting with the blue and completing the pattern.
9. Do the brown zig-zag outline. Starting from the center and working around.
10. Start the border motifs with the orange outlines on both sides of the zig-zag.
11. Complete motifs and remaining details.
12. Blue and yellow border.
13. Brown border, worked over three threads for a corded look.
14. The middle background in sand.
15. The second background in green.
16. The outer background on the edge in sand.

SIZE: 14″x 14″

TOP

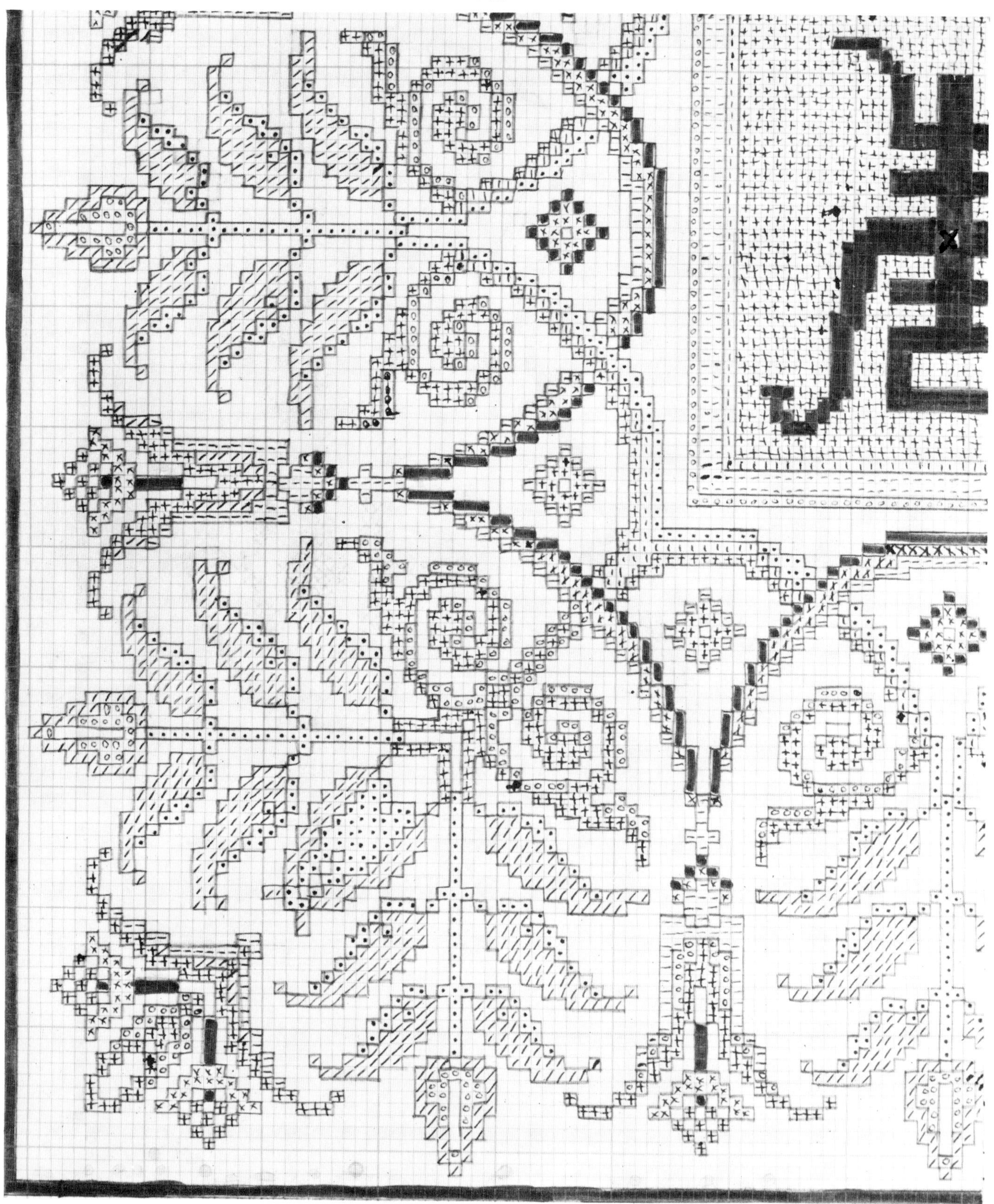

COLORS:

- Purple
- Lavender
- Red
- Gold
- Yellow
- Dark Brown
- Light Brown
- Light Green

White background

"PEKING AUTUMN"

1. Mark the canvas top with TOP.
2. Begin your center motif in purple from the center of the canvas.
3. Start your border around the oriental pattern, in light green.
4. Follow with two rows of red, one of gold.
5. Fill the background inside this border in yellow.
6. Next do the purple outline.
7. Now dot the dark brown outlines.
8. Do the other outlines.
9. Complete the border.
10. Do the purple border edge over three threads.
11. White background.

SIZE: 16″x 16″

TOP

COLORS:

- Red
- Yellow
- Black
- White

"DRAGON"

1. Mark your canvas on top with TOP.
2. Start with the yellow design in the middle. Notice that the top design is different than the lower one. Do all the yellow outlining first.
3. Outline the black Dragon first, starting from the tail, closest to the yellow center. You will have two Dragons facing you, with a yellow center and a yellow motif under each Dragon. Fill in the Dragon.
4. Do the black center border.
5. Now complete the border in white.
6. Finish the center background in red.
7. Do the bottom border, the same as above.
8. Start the outside border with the red.
9. Now the black on both sides.
10. Complete border.

SIZE: 11″x 13″

COLORS:

- ⊡ Green
- ■ Brown
- ◪ Yellow
- ⊠ Cream
- ◙ Beige

"ACORN"

1. Begin the brown outline from the center.
2. Yellow center design.
3. From the yellow design complete the pattern.
4. Center brown border.
5. Fill in background in cream.
6. Do the brown motifs and completing the motif with the cream squares.
7. From the cream square start the yellow leaves.
8. Complete the centers.
9. Brown and cream border.
10. The inside of this border has a green background.

SIZE: 16½"x 16½"

INDEX

BY TITLE

BY SIZE

BY INFLUENCE

ABOUT THE AUTHOR

SYLVIA GOLDMAN was born Sofia Pedroza in Mexico City. Both her parents performed in American movies, and her father, Alfonso Pedroza, became a well-known opera singer and played the role of Diego Rivera in the Broadway show *Mexican Hayride.*

Sylvia first studied the arts and crafts as a child while attending convent schools in Los Angeles, where she was taught knitting, crochet, needlepoint, sewing, painting, and sculpture. As a teenager, she continued her studies in art and design, planning to become a dress designer. While going to school, she worked in several movie studios, including MGM, Columbia, and Paramount.

At eighteen, while on a visit to her father who was then appearing on Broadway, she met Murray Goldman; after a whirlwind courtship they were married. Setting her career plans aside, she settled down in Great Neck, Long Island, to raise a family of five children. While the youngsters were growing up, she studied painting with Esphyr Slobodinka. In her spare time she designs and sews all her clothing, and she enjoys tennis and gourmet cooking.

She was re-introduced to needlepoint when her oldest daughter, hospitalized with leukemia, received the gift of a needlepoint kit from a friend. After she and her daughter completed their first pillow, Sylvia took every opportunity to increase her knowledge of this craft, and went on to design patterns for friends and family. Her designs blend a highly original talent with a rich family and cultural background that includes Indian, French, Italian, English, and Spanish ancestry.

Following her daughter's death, she adapted her designs in graph form for publication, donating the proceeds to leukemia research in her daughter's name.